# HORRIBLE HISTORIES

# WICKED
# WORDS

DISCARDED

Terry Deary

SCHOLAS

For Barbara Allen, with thanks

Scholastic Children's Books,
Euston House, 24 Eversholt Street,
London NW1 1DB, UK

A division of Scholastic Ltd
London ~ New York ~ Toronto ~ Sydney ~ Auckland
Mexico City ~ New Delhi ~ Hong Kong

First published in the UK by Scholastic Ltd, 1996
This edition published 2017

ISBN 978 1407 18570 5

Page layout services provided by Quadrum Solutions Ltd, Mumbai, India
Printed and bound in the UK by CPI Group (UK) Ltd, Croydon, CR0 4YY

4 6 8 10 9 7 5 3

# CONTENTS

**Introduction** 5

**Timeline** 10

Awful Anglo-Saxons 13

Blood and butchery 17

Chaucer's chicken 24

Clever Caxton 29

Daft Definitions 31

Deadly Dickens 41

Euseful euphemism 46

Farcical figures of speech 54

Fascinating foreign languages 61

Groovy games with wicked words 63

Gruesome grammar 72

Hocus pocus 74

Ice-cool invaders 77

Interesting initials 80

Jolly jargon 83

Jesting Johnson 89

Knock-knock 92

Lousy Latin 95
Muddled Mrs Malaprop 96
Nasty Normans 99
Odd onomatopoeia 105
Potty proverbs 107
Quaint qabbalah 114
Rotten riddles 117
Renaissance 124
Superstar Shakespeare 127
Snooty snobs 132
Suffering spelling 136
Slobbish slang 142
Shocking swear words 145
Silly Spooner 149
Terrible tongue-twisters 153
United States of America 156
Vile verse 163
Wicked words to test your teacher 169
X-words 176
Y-drunken 180
Zee end ... or is it? 181
**Interesting index** 190

# Introduction

### Word power

People say some daft things. 'Sticks and stones may break my bones but words can never hurt me,' they say.

'That's balderdash,' I say.[1] Here are some words that might hurt...

So words can be quite, quite wicked. Wicked weapons. Baron Lytton even went so far as to say, 'The pen is mightier than the sword.'

1 To be honest it isn't *really* balderdash – because *balderdash* was a type of cheap and nasty wine – but you know what I mean.

Throughout history words have meant POWER. From the mid 1300s you could escape being hanged if you could read aloud the first verse of the 51st Psalm. This proved you were 'educated' and you could get away with murder ... or to be accurate you got away with having your left thumb branded. (Though if you committed a *second* hanging crime then you went to the gallows even if you could read the whole of the Bible backwards.)

Reciting this 'neck verse' was scrapped in 1705 when it was realized uneducated villains learned the words by heart! Alas, the ability to read no longer works in escaping punishment...

There's only one way to get your hands on this amazing power of words. Know more about words than anyone else in the world! Read this book and you can know more than anyone in the entire universe! (Oh, I forgot to mention ... words also give you the power to exaggerate a bit.)

## In the beginning...

'In the beginning was the Word ...' At least, that's what the Bible says. But of course we don't actually know *what that word was.*

Somebody can probably tell you what *your* first word was. When you sat on your newly filled nappy and said, 'Pooh!' your adoring mother probably looked at your proud father and said, 'Oh, darling. It said its first word!'

But what about the very first word of all? It's not as if some prehistoric human said, 'Unk!' then stopped, looked at its mates and said, 'Hey guys! I've just said the first word ... ever!'

We can only *guess* the sort of things those early speakers talked about from the way they ran their lives. Intelligent human-like apes called 'Neanderthals', were the first creatures to wear clothes, make weapons and bury their dead. Piles of animal bones showed that they ate anything they could get their hairy hands on. If they had language then it must have been dead simple.

Then along came a newer ape called *Homo sapiens*. Look at *their* piles of old animal bones and what do you notice? They are much more *organized*. Bison in one season, deer in the next and so on. How did they *do* that? They must have been able to use words to say things like,

What happened next? Neanderthals died out, *Homo sapiens* survived and became people. People like you and me ... only a bit *uglier* than *me*. (I don't know about you.) That was the power of words. They were the difference between survival and extinction. (If dinosaurs could have talked then you might have been turning these pages with your prehensile tail.)

The power of words probably allowed *Homo sapiens* grown-ups to pass on their wisdom to their children. Imagine it. With the power of words came the power of *teaching*. The first teachers were probably language teachers – and they're *still* at it.

Of course it was a couple of million years before humans got around to inventing writing. Among the first things they wrote were the things that had happened to them. They invented that other horrible subject ... History!

So Wicked Words and Horrible History go together – and here they are for the first time in one book.

# Timeline

AD **43–410** Romans rule Britain. The native Brits speak Celtic. The Romans speak Latin. The Romans disappear, leaving behind a few of their wicked words and …

**449** Angles invade the southern part of Britain and make it Angle-land … England. Their language is called Old English. It would look like Old Gobbledegook to most people today.

**787** Vikings invade the north and east of England and add some of their own wicked words until …

**1066** Normans invade from France and their lords speak French but … the peasants still speak English (and the pheasants just squawk).

**1150** The beginnings of Middle English – a mix of Old English and French that you could recognize today … just about.

**1387** A poet called Geoffrey Chaucer begins to write *The Canterbury Tales* – it's a long story poem (with some very rude bits!) and it's written in English.

**1399** Henry IV is the first monarch for over 300 years whose native language is English – very handy. Now he can say useful things like, 'Pay me taxes,' and 'Pay me more taxes.'

**1450** Johannes Gutenberg invents the printing press in Germany – maybe!

_Timeline_

(Some say he pinched the idea
from a Dutchman called Coster.)
He publishes the first printed
Bible. He dies a poor man which
probably serves him right. But …

**1476** Englishman William Caxton
pinches Gutenberg's idea (they're
all at it) and sets up his own printing
press. He starts to spell words in a
regular way. More people can
afford books … but most people
can't actually read them, of course.

**1590** William Shakespeare begins
writing his plays and poems.
Teachers will tell you he's the
greatest English writer ever but he
certainly had problems with
spelling. He's popular with
Elizabethan audiences because his
plays have lots of bloodthirsty
murders and his comedies have
lots of rude jokes – teachers usually
skip over those bits!

**1607** English pilgrims begin to
settle in America and start to make
their language the new language of
North America. The Native
American Indians already have
languages, of course, but the new
settlers prefer English.

**1714** German George becomes
King of England but never learns to
speak English. No one cares. He has
nothing interesting to say anyway.

**1721** The first English dictionary
is produced. Now that ever-

popular children's game is possible – the one called 'spelling tests'.

**1755** Doctor Johnson creates a really good English dictionary – but sadly without any rude words!

**1880** School is compulsory for every child in Britain up until the age of 10. Everyone will be taught to read and write … whether they like it or not!

**1937** A Dictionary of English Slang is published. Some of the words are thought so shocking it is banned from many library shelves!

**1987** The British Government invents the National Curriculum. Everyone is urged to write and speak 'The Queen's English' – wicked, eh?

# Awful Anglo-Saxons

## Horrible history of the language – part 1

Every time Britain has been invaded the invaders have brought something with them – dirty great weapons, a mean attitude ... and a packed lunch. They have also brought their *language*. If they could force their language on the natives of these islands then they had won. Language has been used like a football for booting the British ...

**1** The prehistoric home team in the British Isles were the Celts ... unfortunately they didn't play together very well. In fact they even had the odd scrap amongst themselves.

**2** The first visiting team was the Roman Army. They were a well organized side. They soon drove the Celts back into their penalty area – Wales and Scotland.

PERSONALLY I PREFER THE 4-4-2 SYSTEM...

**3** The Romans had crowd trouble back in Italy and left. Before the Celtic defence could recover the next visitors, the Angles and Saxons from Germany, were on the attack.

**4** The Angles won and decided to make Britain their home ground. They changed the name to Angle-land – that's England to you – and made Angle-ish (English) the language of their supporters.

Celtic languages are still spoken in Scotland, Ireland, Wales and Brittany (Western France) by about half a million people. Surprisingly there are very few Celtic words left in the English language. There are words like *cross*, *crag*, *bin* and *brock* (for badger) and some place names like the rivers *Thames*, *Avon* and *Exe*, the county of *Kent* and the town of *Dover*.

The Angles were great *fighters* but not great *writers*. We don't have much of a record of their language until the Romans came back. The Christian missionary from Rome, St Augustine, landed in Kent in AD 597 and his mate, Pope Gregory the Great, cracked the first English joke.

HEALTH WARNING: This joke needs a bit of explaining. Any joke that needs explaining can't be very good.

To be honest, old Pope Greg said it in Latin. His actual words were, 'Non Angli sed Angeli' ... but it still doesn't get into the Top Ten of All-Time Great Jokes. Of course, it *has* been remembered after 1400 years and that's quite an achievement.

The monks also brought about 500 Latin words with them that we still use today ... If it wasn't for them we wouldn't be able to say ...

And talking about memorable Old English words, that brings us neatly on to ...

# Blood and butchery

Those Old English enjoyed nothing better than a good horror story – plenty of blood and plenty of butchery. They used wicked words in clever ways to make the hair stand up on the back of your tonsils. They were so clever that we still use those word-tricks today. Tricks like ...

## Amazing alliteration

FRED FLOOGLE FRIES FIFTY FISH FOR FRIDAY FEAST!

GARY GRINT GRABS GREAT GOAL!

CLODHOPPING CLIFF CLIMBER CARELESSLY CRUSHES KING CRAB'S CLAW!

NINETY NOBLE KNIGHTS KNEEL NEATLY

You can see that each of the words in each headline begins with the same sound. Teachers have a fancy name for this ... alliteration.

Many comic and cartoon characters *alliterate* ... **Donald Duck, Mickey Mouse, Fred Flintstone** and so on. You can probably think of a hundred others.

Names that *alliterate* stick in your memory. Everyone remembers **King Kong** ... they might have forgotten him if he was called King Jungle-ape or Gorilla Kong. People who invent adverts want their ads to stick in your mind so they often use alliteration too. A supermarket called **P**resto claimed they were '**P**roud of our **p**eople, **p**roud of our **p**rices.' And book writers think of silly titles like *Horrible Histories – Wicked Words*!

Back in the Dark Ages (AD 450 to AD 1000) when people couldn't read, *alliteration* came in very handy. Suppose you were a poet. You travelled from castle to castle and sang your poems for the lord and his guests. You sang for your supper. You must *not* forget your words! And poems of 3,000 lines were common.

Today many poets make their lines *rhyme* – the ends of the lines sound the same – but the Dark Age poems *alliterated*. It must have worked because the poems went on for *hours!* No television in those days, remember.

The other wicked thing about the poems was that they were gruesomely gory. Eventually some people (usually monks) wrote a few of these poems down. That's how we know about them now. One of the most famously horrible poems was about a warrior called Beowulf – a super-hero. Here's his two-hour tale, retold in a few lines by a group of children, and using modern English words but using Old English *alliteration* …

HEALTH WARNING: Reading stories like this can give you nightmares!

### Beowulf

> *Beowulf's brave brothers feasted by the fierce fires,*
> *    then snored*
> *While their courageous captain guarded the gate.*
> *The grinning Grendel crept through a secret side door*
> *And the terrible beast crushed and cracked a man.*
> *While most men slept the gruesome Grendel*
> *    slid into the hall.*
> *He tore thirty men apart.*
> *Bloody rivers ran down the walls.*
> *The grouching Grendel turned to see the*
> *    unarmed Beowulf.*
> *The hero bit and pulled the greasy Grendel's arm off.*
> *The menacing muscular men woke and drove the*
> *    ruby-blood-dripping Grendel*
> *To his grave in the ghastly swamp.*

IT'S ALRIGHT LADS – HE'S ARMLESS!

The story does *not* have a happy ending though. Grendel's mother is a bit upset at her son's death; in an underwater fight Beowulf kills her too. However, in a fight with a dragon, Beowulf is finally killed. Or, if we want to alliterate …

# BRAVE BEOWULF BUTCHERS BEAST BUT BECOMES BAKED BY BIGGER BREATH BURNER

(Try saying that with a mouth full of mushrooms!)

### Gruesome Gawain

A great 14th-century poet created a horrific epic, *Sir Gawain and the Green Knight* – we don't know the poet's name but around the year 1350 he wrote his grippingly gruesome poem.

KING ARTHUR WAS CELEBRATING CHRISTMAS AT CAMELOT WITH HIS KNIGHTS OF THE ROUND TABLE WHEN A GIANT STRANGER ENTERED THE HALL....

HE'S ALL GREEN! EVEN HIS HAIR!

THE STRANGER GAVE OUT A CHALLENGE...

I WILL STAND ANY BLOW YOUR CHAMPION CAN GIVE ME!

ANY?

AND HE GAVE HIS CONDITIONS...

ALL I ASK IS THAT I CAN HAVE A FREE BLOW IN RETURN, A YEAR FROM NOW!

THEN I ACCEPT THE CHALLENGE

SIR GAWAIN STEPPED FORWARD, RAISED HIS SWORD, AND CUT THE GREEN KNIGHT'S HEAD CLEAN OFF HIS BODY....

SEE YOU NEXT YEAR!

SNIK

BUT TO EVERYONE'S HORROR THE KNIGHT PICKED UP HIS HEAD

I WILL RETURN ONE YEAR FROM NOW!

AND HE HEADED OFF HOME!

SIR GAWAIN SEARCHED THE LAND FOR THE GREEN KNIGHT...

...UNTIL HE REACHED A LONELY CASTLE

SIR GAWAIN WAS BEFRIENDED BY THE LADY OF THE CASTLE

TAKE MY BELT-IT WILL PROTECT YOU WHEN YOU MEET THE GREAT GREEN KNIGHT

AND WHEN THEY MET ON A MISTED MOOR, THE GREEN KNIGHT SWUNG HIS SWORD..

...BUT GAWAIN'S BELT PROTECTED HIM.

THE MEN SHOOK HANDS AND PARTED FRIENDS. THEN GAWAIN RODE BACK HOME TO CAMELOT...

"IT SEEMS THE LADY WAS THE GREEN KNIGHT'S WIFE, REPAID MY KINDNESS WHEN SHE SAVED MY LIFE!"

## Pathetic Piers

Other great poets made English poetry popular in the 14th century. One was called William Langland. He wrote a poem called the *Vision of Piers Plowman*, a gruelling account of life for peasants ...

> *The needy are our neighbours, if we note rightly;*
> *They have woe in the winter time, and wake at*
>    *midnight*
> *To rise and rock the cradle at the bedside.*
> *The woe of these women who dwell in hovels*
> *Is too sad to speak of or to say in rhyme.*

Meanwhile the ploughman's wife was ...

> *Wrapped in a floor cloth to keep out the weather*
> *She was barefoot on bare ice, until her feet bled.*

Cheerful stuff! But the poem was popular with the poor peasants. The peasants couldn't *read* but they *remembered* long chunks of Langland's poetry.

In 1381 the peasants tried to revolt against their lords and one of their leaders, a priest called John Ball, used Langland's poem to stir up the peasants. The power of the word again!

THE PEASANTS ARE REVOLTING!

OH, SHUT UP!

HEALTH WARNING: Quoting poetry can damage your health. It did Ball no good. He was captured, hanged, tortured and cut up – wicked!

## Victorian viciousness

The popular Victorian opera writers, Gilbert and Sullivan, used alliteration for more gruesome effect in their 1885 comic opera, *The Mikado*. A character sighs as he waits for his trial and execution ...

> *To sit in solemn silence in a dull, dark dock,*
> *In pestilential prison with a life-long lock,*
> *Awaiting the sensation of a short, sharp shock,*
> *From a cheap and chippy chopper on a big black*
>    *block!*

Around a hundred years later, a government minister pinched Gilbert and Sullivan's alliteration to describe what he was going to do to young criminals in future. He said the courts would give offenders a 'short, sharp shock'. (A tough prison life ... not an axe on the back of the neck!) That politician *had* to use alliteration, of course, because his name was ... Willie Whitelaw!

*Did you know...?*
The English cricketer, Freddy Trueman, once said, 'People started calling me *fiery* because *fiery* rhymes with *Fred* the way *Typhoon* rhymes with *Tyson*' – the name of the fast bowler. Of course, he meant that the names alliterate.

# Chaucer's chicken

Langland and the writer of Gawain wrote their poems in the old English 'alliterative' style, but they also ended each verse with two rhyming lines ... like the last two lines in the Gawain story:

> *It seems the lady was the Green Knight's wife,*
> *Repaid my kindness when she saved my life!*

The Old English poetry gradually made way for the rhyming style we know today. The third of the great 14th-century poets, Geoffrey Chaucer, used the pairs of rhyming lines for all of his poems. Chaucer was born in London in the first half of the 1340s ... and was lucky to escape the Black Death that killed half the people in England between 1348 and 1349.

He travelled through Europe and collected a lot of good stories. Chaucer also came up with a clever idea to link all the stories into one long poem. He imagined a group of travellers riding to Canterbury on a holy pilgrimage. As they rode along, each traveller in turn told a story. The collection of stories became *The Canterbury Tales.*

Some tales are funny, some are creepy and some are very rude! The stories are good, as you'll see, but *The Canterbury Tales* are important because they were the first tales to be written in an English that we can just about recognize today. Here's an example from *The Nun's Priest's Tale*.

| Chaucer | Modern English |
|---|---|
| *A poure wydwe, somdel stape in age,* | A poor widow, quite advanced in age, |
| *Was whilom dwellyng in a narwe cotage,* | Was once dwelling in a small cottage, |
| *Beside a greve, stondynge in a dale* | Beside a wood standing in a dale |
| *This wydwe, of which I telle yow my tale,* | This widow, of which I tell you my tale, |
| *Syn thilke day that she was last a wyf* | Since that same day she was last a wife |
| *In pacience ladded a ful symple lyf* | In patience led a full simple life |

25

See? Some words are exactly the same as ours (age, beside, tale) some are almost the same (dwellyng, telle, wyf) and some you can work out – narwe is like narrow – small. Simple isn't it?

But let's get on with the story in a modern English version. This widow had a cockerel called Chanticleer, and the story is really about him and his close encounter with a local chicken-chewer …

*A black-faced fox, so evil and so sly,*
*Had lived three years there in the woods close by.*
*And, by a fine and very cunning plot,*
*One night into widow's yard had got*
*Then, in the warm sun, Chanticleer so free*
*Sang merrier than a mermaid in the sea.*

*The fox said, 'Noble sir, ah, please don't go.*
*Be not afraid of me. I am no foe!*
*I plan no hurt. I mean no villainy.*
*I came not to disturb your privacy.*
*I came into this yard for just one thing.*
*I came to hear your angel-sweet voice sing!'*

*So Chanticleer stood high upon his toes,*
*He stretched his neck, he made his eyes to close.*
*He launched a crow so loud and clear of sound ...*
*Sir Russell Fox leapt on him with a bound!*
*And by the throat he seized this Chanticleer;*
*He flung him on his back and sped from here.*

*The simple widow and her daughters two*
*Heard all the hens cry with a great to-do.*
*The village men and women joined the chase;*
*They yelled like fiends from hell as they did race.*
*The came with horns of bone, they blew, they tooted,*
*They screamed, they shrieked, they roared, they*
*        whooped and hooted.*

*The cockerel on the fox's back he lay,*
*Despite his fear he found the voice to say,*
*'If I were you I'd turn and face the crowd.*
*I'd curse them, mock them, laugh at them aloud.*
*Tell how you'll eat me, how they'll not catch you!'*
*The fox replied, 'In faith that's what I'll do!'*

*But as he spoke, his open mouth set free*
*The crafty cockerel, who flew to a tree.*
*The fox had lost the dinner he had earned.*
*For him, and Chanticleer, a lesson learned.*
*And you, take warning, now my tale is sung.*
*Don't jabber when you ought to hold your tongue.*

27

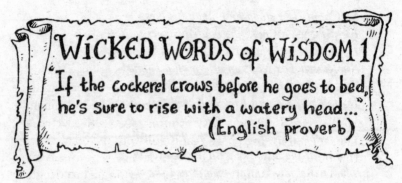

WICKED WORDS of WISDOM 1
If the cockerel crows before he goes to bed,
he's sure to rise with a watery head...
(English proverb)

Get it? No? He'll rise with a watery head means it will rain before morning.

# Clever Caxton

Chaucer wrote his *Canterbury Tales* in the 1390s. Within 90 years another man had just as great an effect on the English language. And he wasn't a writer! In 1476 William Caxton set up England's first printing press and started a fashion for publishing books that is still with us today.

But he had problems. There were lots of ways of saying the same thing in Middle English, so Caxton had to decide which ones to use. He gave an example of his problems with a story in one of his books …

And sure as eggs is eggs, Caxton was right. What did he do? He chose one word with one spelling and stuck with it in every book. In time, everyone began to follow Caxton's spelling.

We had the start of 'Standard' English and the start of Modern English. William Caxton. What a man!

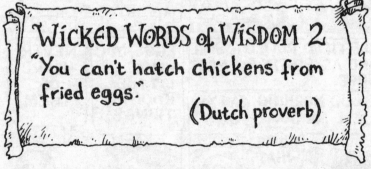

This is probably double-Dutch to most people but it's something to do with eating something small now (a fried egg) or eating better if you wait a while (and have roast chicken). In other words, be patient!

# Daft Definitions

Some words have stories attached to them rather like fleas have dogs attached to them. Here's an alphabet of wicked words. BUT ... one of these stories is a complete invention. Can you spot the one that's a lie?

**A Adder** The snake was never meant to be an *adder*. All those jokes about it being good at sums will have to be forgotten. The Middle English name was *naddre*. Then along came some clever-clogs with a pen and said, 'What's that snake?' The reply was, 'A naddre.' 'An adder! Thank you,' and off he went. And, I'll bet you didn't know, the Old English buzzing, stinging insect was a *waps* until someone twisted its tail and made it into a *wasp*. Even an Old English *bridd* became a *bird*. How would *you* like to be called by the wrong name for the rest of time?

**B Black Maria** This, if you don't know, is a police van for taking criminals to prison. The story is that Maria Lee lived in a run-down part of Boston, USA, in the 1830s. When the police wagon came round the streets, Maria, who was a strong black American, would help load the troublemakers onto it. So when the police wanted help they sent for Black Maria.

**C Calculate** The Romans did not have calculators. If they wanted to count then they ran out of fingers and toes when they reached 20 – a one-legged war hero would run out even sooner! So they used pebbles as counters. The Latin word for pebble was *calculus*. Next time teacher asks you to 'calculate' two and two then pick a pile of pebbles from your pocket …

**D Dismal** This word comes from two Latin words – *dies* and *mali* – meaning days and evil. So *dismal* means evil days. In the Middle Ages people believed two days in each month were unlucky. So beware 1, 25 January, 2, 26 February, 1, 28 March, 10, 20 April, 3, 25 May, 10, 16 June, 13, 22 July, 1, 30 August, 3, 21 September, 3, 22 October, 5, 28 November, 7, 22 December. You may like to stay off school on those days and avoid getting *dismal* marks.

**E Egress** This word means the same as 'Exit' (so you could say it's a pretty *way out* word). Not many people know that. So an American showman called Phineas Barnum used it when he had problems with visitors. Some stayed too long watching his shows, so new customers couldn't get in till they

left. This delay was costing Phineas their entrance money. So he put up a sign saying *To the Egress*. People moved along to see this strange creature, the *egress*. What was it? A female eagle perhaps? When they found themselves outside they found out just what *egress* meant!

**F Ferret** How would you like to go through life being called *thief*? That's what ferrets do. Their name comes from the Latin word *fur* which means thief. Just because these cute, little, fluffy, over-stretched hamsters dive into the burrows of other creatures and ferret about seeing what they can find. They're probably only pinching a baby bunny-rabbit for supper. If there was a McFerret Burger Bar they'd probably sell *Bunny in a Bun* and the poor ferrets wouldn't *have* to thieve.

**G Gift** You probably enjoy getting a gift (or 20) at Christmas. But the word didn't always mean a *free present*. In Old

English a *gift* was something a man gave as a payment for a wife! Beware, girls … if a young man gives your father a *gift* just make sure he isn't paying to marry you.

**H Hooligan** If anyone ever calls you a 'hooligan' then you should probably sue them. You might just be compared to a criminal from Ireland called Patrick Hooligan. He gave the London police a hard time in the 1890s.

**I Infantry** The word means *foot soldiers* these days. But before the 16th century it meant the soldiers who were too young to fight with the horse soldiers (the *cavalry*). The word comes from the Italian word *infante* or boy. We call very young children *infants*. It's important to know the difference between *infants* and *infantry*. Remember, infantry are trained not to hurt their friends, whereas infants are quite brutal little savages …

**J Jerry** Before people had indoor toilets they had large pots in case they needed the toilet in the middle of the night. This pot was originally known as a *jeroboam* – and the name became shortened to *Jerry*. During the First World War (1914–1918) the British soldiers looked at the helmets of the German soldiers and thought they looked like *Jerry* pots. They called the Germans *Jerries*. (Some boring people try to say that *Jerry* is simply short for German.)

WITH THESE NEW DUAL PURPOSE HELMETS WE SHALL CONQUER THE WORLD!

**K Knickerbockers** These baggy trousers, gathered in at the knee, have nothing to do with knickers. A writer called Washington Irving wrote stories of old New York and pretended that they were written by an old Dutch settler – Diedrich Knickerbocker. Old Dutch settlers wore the baggy trousers so the trousers became known as *knickerbockers*. In the same way, the Duke of Wellington wore high boots – so high boots became known as *wellingtons*. The Earl of Sandwich liked bread round his meat – bread round meat became known as *sandwiches*. The difference is that Wellington and Sandwich really existed – Dietrich Knickerbocker was just an invented name.

**L Leg** At one time this was considered to be a rude word! The Victorians believed a polite lady would never let a man see her legs. In time they didn't even dare to use the word. They preferred the word *limb*.

There is even a story that in some Victorian houses the legs (sorry, *limbs*) of furniture would be decently clothed in little trousers. This story was possibly a joke yet many people will swear that it's true.

**M Mascot** The word is borrowed from the Italian *masco* meaning 'little witch'. They bring lucky magic to a person, a group of people or a team.

**N Nostalgia** Most people use this to mean 'having a longing for the past'. In fact the Greek words *nostos* and *algos* mean *return home* and *pain*. To be exact, a *nostalgic* person is really a *homesick* person. Most people are nostalgic in that sense – at some time or another we all get sick of home.

**O Oscar** Every year the Academy of Motion Picture Arts and Sciences in the USA award prizes for the best films, actors, directors, and so on, in their industry. This began in 1929 when the gold-plated statues were handed out as trophies. Then, in 1932, the Librarian of the Academy was heard to say, 'Gee, those statues remind me of my Uncle Oscar!' A newspaper reporter heard her and printed the story. From that day on the trophies have been known as *Oscars*.

**P Pneumonoultramicroscopicsilicovolcanoconiosis** With 45 letters it's the longest word in the Oxford English Dictionary. It describes a lung condition suffered by some miners. It leaves them short of breath ... not just the disease, but trying to tell their friends what's the matter with them. If you enjoy saying long words then there's a word for that too – a little word with only 32 letters – you are into *hippopotomonstrosesquipedalianism*.

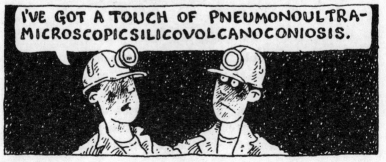

**Q Quiz** James Daly was a theatre manager in Dublin in 1782. He once had a bet with a friend that he could introduce a new word into the English language in a day. He then had the word *quiz* chalked on all the walls of the city. Everyone who saw it began talking about it. Daly won the bet ... and we have a fairly useful word. This seems an unlikely story – but no dictionary has a better explanation! (The origins of this word would make a good quiz question come to think of it.)

**R Robot** The Czech playwright, Karel Capek, invented the word *robot* in one of his plays to mean 'mechanical slave'. Next time teacher orders you to clean the blackboard then you can rightly grumble, 'He must think I'm a robot!'

**S Sideburns** A man who grows whiskers down the side of his face is said to grow *sideburns*. In fact the word became popular when these whiskers were grown by a US General and sort of named after him. But his name wasn't Sideburn ... it was Burnside! Somehow the two halves of his name became mixed up. Sideburns became popular in the 1960s again. Sometimes the word becomes totally twisted into *sideboards* ... and a sideboard can also be a cabinet you keep your china in!

**T Taxi** Some words have travelled a long way to arrive at where they are now. *Taxai* was a Greek word which the Romans pinched and changed to *taxare* – that meant to 'reckon'. In 1890 a German invented a machine to *reckon* the cost of a journey – he borrowed the Roman word and called his machine a *taxameter*. The French borrowed the name and called the machine a *taximetre*. The English borrowed the words from the French and called both the machine and the vehicle a *taxy*. In time this changed to *taxi*. *Taxai* to *taxi* took about 3,000 years. The gallant little word tried to cross the Atlantic … but seems to have sunk on the way. The Americans call it a *cab*!

**U Umbrella** As you know, *umber* is a shade of brown. Eleanor (wife of King Henry III and *Ella* for short) was very brown from riding in the sun too much. People used to comment on it as she rode through London. 'There goes umber Ella,' they would shout. So Ella invented a sunshade to keep the sun's rays off her face. Children watched her riding with this thing over her head and said, 'What's that, mum?' The parents replied, 'That's just umber-Ella.' The kids thought they were talking about the sun shade and the name stuck.

**V Vaccination** Ever been *vaccinated* against a disease? Ever wondered where the name *vaccination* comes from? Probably not. Probably better if you don't know, come to think of it. So, I won't tell you that it comes from the Latin *vacca* for cow. Edward Jenner noticed that people who had suffered from 'cow pox' never suffered from the deadlier 'small pox'. So clever Ed gave people cow pox (or *vacca* pox) to stop them getting small pox. Think of those poor people being injected with infected cow juices and stop whingeing about a little prick of a needle. It could be *worse*!

**W We** This word means 'you and I' or 'these people and I'. But some people use it instead of 'I'. Kings and queens have often used 'we' instead of 'I'. A famous example is Queen Victoria, who was supposed to have said 'We are not amused.' (Old Vic never actually said or wrote those particular words, but that's another story!) As a result it is

TIME FOR A ROYAL WEE...

known as the 'Royal We' when it's used this way. If you aren't a monarch and you use the 'Royal We' then you risk being laughed at. The British Prime Minister, Margaret Thatcher, was a figure of fun when her son had a child and she announced, 'We have become a grandmother!'

**X X-rays** A German scientist discovered some mysterious rays in 1895. He didn't know quite what they were so he called them X because, in mathematics, X means 'unknown'. Now, if you break a bone you will probably have an X-ray. Imagine that. Something 'unknown' passing through your body! Creepy, eh?

**Y Yuppie** If you are a Young, Urban (live in a town), Professional Person then you are a YUPPie. The word was thought up in the 1980s to describe this class of people. Other words have grown in a similar way. A married couple who both work may be Double-Income-No-Kids – DINKies. With any luck you could grow up to be a Person-Inheriting-Parents'-Property (a PIPPie) and grow old gracefully into a Well-Off-Older-Person (or WOOPie). A Russian Yuppie is a Yupsky and a Japanese Yuppie is a Juppie ... but whatever you do, and however much money you make, try not to become a LOMBARD! Lots-Of-Money-But-A-Right-Dipstick.

**Z Zzzzz** Sometimes people write lists of wickedly interesting words. Others make you want to zzzzz!

*Answer:* Did you spot the one description that is nonsense? Not easy because many of the true explanations are hard to believe! In fact the one fake is 'U for umbrella'. The word comes from the Italian for little shade and has nothing to do with a sun-burned woman called Ella!

*Did you know...?*
Some clever person worked out that *smiled* is probably the longest word in the world ... but why? Answer: Because there is a mile between the first letter and the last. Boom-boom!

# Deadly Dickens

## Dickens's dead ducks

Charles Dickens (1812–70) was a very popular writer in Victorian times – even though he said some very nasty things about the Victorians! He was very much against hanging people in public, for example. Dickens said that the crowds who gathered to see a hanging were as disgusting as the criminal who was being hanged. In 1846 he wrote to *The Daily News* newspaper …

> *I was present myself at the execution of Courvoisier. I was purposely on the spot from midnight of the night before, and was near witness to the whole process of the building of the scaffold, the gathering of the crowd, the gradual swelling of numbers with the coming of the day, the hanging of the man, the cutting of the body down and the removal of it to prison. From the moment of my arrival I did not see any suitable emotion in any of the immense crowd. No sorrow, no terror, no dislike, no seriousness – nothing but indecency, frivolity, drunkenness and vice in fifty other shapes. I thought it was impossible that I could feel so disgusted by my fellow-creatures.*

With the help of Dickens's writing the hideous spectacle was ended in the 1860s. That's the power of the word again in the hands of a good writer.

The Victorians didn't mind watching a bit of horrible hanging but they were very fussy when it came to *reading* about such things. Dickens had to decide when to shock people and when to leave the horror to their imaginations.

The guillotine is a very messy method of execution, as you can imagine. Quick ... but messy. Blood all over the place.

At the end of his book *A Tale of Two Cities*, Charles Dickens's two characters, a woman and a man, go for the chop. Do we get all the gory details? First the woman steps forward. Dickens writes...

*She goes next before him – is gone.*

That's it! That's all Dickens wrote about her execution. 'Gone.' Gone where? Never mind, perhaps the chopped chap will tell us the plain truth. He is bravely taking the place of another man so that other man can escape. His last words are ...

That's the end. The end of the *whole book*. He's going to *rest!* (The poor bloke will be very disappointed when he wakes up and find his head isn't on the pillow beside him!)

*Did you know…?*
Mix up the letters of Charles Dickens and you get *Rash Neck Sliced* – ideal for the author of *A Tale of Two Cities*.

Dickens leaves the readers with tears running down their legs – sadness rather than horror. But, when he *wants* to horrify us he *can*. In *A Christmas Carol*, when the writer wants to shock Ebenezer Scrooge into changing his wicked ways he shows him a grave…

> *A churchyard. Here then the wretched man (whose name Scrooge had to learn) lay underneath the ground. It was a worthy place. Walled in by houses; overrun by grass and weeds, the growth of vegetation's death, not life; choked up with too much burying.*

43

*The Spirit stood among the graves and pointed down to one.*

*Scrooge crept towards it, trembling as he went; and following the finger, read upon the stone of the neglected grave his own name, Ebenezer Scrooge.*

Great stuff! And the villainous Bill Sykes in *Oliver Twist* has a gruesome end when he hangs himself and his dog *dashed out his brains.* Wicked!

Dickens also managed to get a few 'messages' into his stories. When the character Fagin is about to be executed in *Oliver Twist*, Charles Dickens paints a picture in words of the sheer disgusting spectacle of a public execution. He used his story to repeat what he had written in his letter to the newspaper …

*A great multitude had already assembled; the windows were filled with people, smoking and playing cards to pass the time; the crowd were pushing, quarrelling, joking. Everything told of life, but one dark cluster of objects in the centre of all – the black stage, the cross-beam, the rope and all the hideous apparatus of death.*

So the message is (when you're writing your classic) that the goodies 'go to rest' while the baddies face the 'hideous apparatus of death'.

Now there is a word for words that avoid nastiness. Euphemism ...

# Euseful Euphemism

If it sounds all Greek to you then that's probably because it *is* all Greek. The word comes from the Greek words *eu* (meaning good) and *pheme* (meaning speech). Good speech, or pleasant speech, to soften the blow of something nasty or *un*pleasant. If you have something nasty to say then you may use *euphemism* to say it.

If someone tells you, 'My parrot has hopped the twig,' then don't think the feathered fiend has flown away. It has *died*.

If your friend tells you, 'I need the little girl's room,' then she wants a *toilet*, not a Wendy house.

Euphemisms aren't 20th-century inventions. People have used them for thousands of years. They probably started with religion. Superstitious people didn't want to offend the great spirit of the heavens by calling Him by His name … God. Usually they called Him by His title … Lord. (Rather as you might be afraid to call an awesome teacher by his name – Mister Popplesniff – you'd call him, Sir.)

By the Middle Ages people were still afraid to swear something in God's name. They swore *by his nails*, or *by the blood of Christ*, or *by God's precious heart*. These are all mentioned in Chaucer's poems.

But the Victorians were probably the best at avoiding unpleasant or naughty words. No one but a Victorian would call certain clothes 'unmentionables'. (I'd tell you what they are – but I'm afraid they're unmentionable.) If a Victorian needed to use the potty in the bedroom during the night then they'd politely use the *gezunda* – because it goes-under (gezunda) the bed.

## How to use euphemism

Here's a quick lesson in polite language …

**1 Don't** go 'in the nude' … go 'in your birthday suit' – a *euphemism* invented in 1731.

**2 Don't** mention the word *bottom* … use the respectable 'bum' a euphemism that has been used since 1387. (Of course, many people still prefer 'bottom', which is itself a euphemism from the 18th century. And you may have a problem in America where a bum is a tramp. Tell an American that English people sit on bums and they may be a little surprised!)

**3 Don't** call your teacher *fat* ... teachers are always 'pleasingly plump'. (In 1995 a schoolgirl in Durham City, England, invented a new *euphemism* for her Maths teacher. She called him 'Mr Blobby'. Unfortunately, although Mr Blobby was a popular television figure of fun, the teacher had no sense of humour. The girl was suspended from school for a week until she apologized!)

**4 Don't** call your parents *misers* because they refuse to increase your pocket money ... children in 1412 would call them 'pinch-pennies' but by 1843 Charles Dickens had invented the charming Mr Scrooge to describe your close-fisted, stingy, cheese-paring, pinch-beak parent who is as 'tight as the paper on the wall'.

**5 Don't** make fun of that *mole* on your sister's nose ... she will tell you it's a 'beauty spot'

Here is a little story with all the nasty bits taken out and *euphemisms* put in their place – and lots of wicked slang words too, of course. But do you recognize it?

**Once upon a time …**
Our heroine was a magnetic twist who was employed as a garbologist by her uppish sisters. She gave them heartburn so they wore the yellow hose.

'You are a gold brick you slug-a-bed,' they told her as they high-hatted it to the ball.

The twist was so miffed she was spitting nails. Then, who should appear, but a full-bodied woman with a wand. She said, 'You have a Friday face!'

'I have the pip,' the twist admitted. 'My sisters have put on the dog and gone to the ball.'

'Don't pipe your eye and throw in the sponge. With my help you shall go to the ball!'

And the pleasingly plump person was good as her word. When the twist arrived at the ball the peacockish sisters were in such a tiff they wanted to give her Larry Dooley and lay her out in lavender.

But the twist set her cap for the swell who was running the ball. She got on the right side of him. 'You're a cheesecake!' he gasped.

'And you're a beefcake,' she sighed.

'Let's tie the knot,' he suggested.

'I am just a cleansing operative with a liquidity crisis,' she admitted.

'Never mind. I'm a gentleman of leisure,' he said.

In no time at all she had cash-and-carried him and they lived happily ever after. The homely sisters lost their doughnuts and then they cashed in their chips, took a last bow, answered the final summons, went west with the great whipper, hopped on the last rattler, rode the pale horse, hopped the twig and went home in a box where they counted worms and pushed up daisies.

Of course the story is better known as *Cinderella*, but you'd guessed that. You probably guessed most of the *euphemisms* too but, in case you are a few sandwiches short of a picnic, here's a little help …

- *twist* – girl (twist and twirl – cockney 19th-century rhyming slang).
- *magnetic* – attractive.
- *garbologist* – cleaner (20th-century USA).
- *wore the yellow hose* – were jealous (17th-century England).
- *gold brick* – shirker (World War II army expression).
- *slug-a-bed* – lazy person (Shakespeare, *Romeo and Juliet* 1595).
- *Friday face* – (16th-century England), gloomy face (because Friday has always been an unlucky day).
- *put on the dog* – act very grandly (1915 English).
- *pipe your eye* – cry (19th-century Cockney rhyming slang).
- *give her Larry Dooley* – beat her up (Australian 1880 after a boxer of that name).
- *lay out in lavender* – flatten (1822 English – people ready for burial were laid in lavender).
- *cheesecake* – beautiful woman (20th-century USA).
- *beefcake* – attractive man (20th-century USA).
- *with a liquidity crisis* – short of cash, poor (20th-century USA).
- *cash and carried* – married (20th-century Cockney rhyming slang).
- *homely* – ugly (in the USA but means 'pleasant' in the UK).
- *lost their doughnuts* – were sick.
- *cashed in their chips … pushed up daisies* – died. (There have always been lots of euphemisms for people who don't want to use that dreadful four-letter word – d-i-e-d!).

## Evil euphemism

Words can be used to lie. Someone can say a harmless thing but mean something rather nasty. They are popular with the armed forces! Here are ten modern *euphemisms*. What do they mean?

| Words | Meaning |
|---|---|
| 1 air support | a) shooting soldiers on your own side |
| 2 a career change opportunity | b) massacring helpless animals |
| 3 friendly fire | c) second hand |
| 4 neutralizing | d) an air disaster |
| 5 previously enjoyed | e) very smelly and poisonous sewage |
| 6 soft targets | f) blowing people to pieces with bombs |
| 7 regulated organic nutrients | g) torturing someone till they obey you |
| 8 aversion therapy | h) assassinating a human nuisance |
| 9 harvesting | i) the sack |
| 10 controlled flight into terrain | j) human beings |

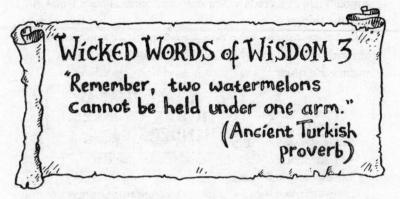

WICKED WORDS of WISDOM 3
"Remember, two watermelons cannot be held under one arm."
(Ancient Turkish proverb)

Meaning? Don't bite off more than you can chew.

# Farcical figures of speech

English has hundreds of 'figures of speech'. That's when you say one thing but mean another. So when teacher tells you to 'Hold your tongue,' she doesn't mean 'Stick your fingers in your mouth and grab hold of that fat slimy thing inside.' She means 'Be quiet.'

IT WAS JUST A FIGURE OF SPEECH, HENDERSON...

Figures of speech cause a lot of trouble to foreigners trying to speak English. They also cause a lot of problems for *British* people trying to speak English! Here are a few old figures of speech ... their meanings and their humorous or horrible history. BUT, beware! One of these explanations is a *lie!* Can you spot the nine true definitions – and the one that is a fake?

**1** *Kick the bucket* – die.
In the Middle Ages a person might have tried to commit suicide by standing on a bucket then tying a noose around their neck with the end of the rope attached to the ceiling above. When they kicked the bucket away they hanged themselves.

I THINK I'M DOING SOMETHING WRONG

**2** *Done in cold blood* – done with no feeling
For thousands of years people (from the Ancient Greeks onward) believed your temper was ruled by the temperature of your blood. A hot-blooded person had a fierce temper, a cold-blooded person had no temper. So, if a cold-blooded person harmed you they did it in a calm, cruel and calculating manner.

A calm and pleasant person didn't have 'hot' blood, of course, so people said, 'Butter wouldn't melt in their mouth'. A figure of speech still used today.

**3** *To be in another person's shoes* – to take someone's place
In the Viking age, when a man adopted a son, the boy accepted by putting on the man's shoes.

**4** *Not worth your salt* – no good
In Roman times salt was a rare and precious mineral – like gold. So it was often used to pay the soldiers. If you weren't *worth* your salt then you didn't *get* your salt – your pay! Of course *salt* comes from a Latin word and people today are still paid a *salary* – a word really meaning *salt*.

55

**5** *Making both ends meet* – having enough money to survive
This is another of those spelling mistakes. In the 19th century business accounts were added up in columns. If the ends of both columns were equal then you had enough money – if they didn't then you were short of money. But the actual word used was *mete* – an old word for equal. So you'd be allright if you made *both ends mete.*

**6** *Having green fingers* – being a talented gardener
The figure of speech is quite simply from the fact that gardeners handle a lot of plants and end up with green stains on their hands. But for some reason, in American English the phrase is *having a green thumb.*

**7** *A forlorn hope* – an impossible dream
This figure of speech had nothing to do with hopes at all! It was taken from the Dutch words *verloren hoop*, which meant *lost troop*. A *verloren hoop* was a sort of suicide squad that was sent ahead of the main forces to attack the enemy. Not many expected to see the *verloren hoop* ever again! If you *did* expect to see them, then it was a pretty *forlorn hope* ... if you see what I mean!

**8** *A narrow escape* – a close experience with disaster
Swiss freedom fighter, William Tell, was captured. His punishment was to fire an arrow at his own son and try to hit an apple perched on his head. If he succeeded then he was free to go. William tell fired the arrow, it brushed his son's hair and split the apple. Whew! 'That was an arrow escape,' his son said. This story was later repeated to a historian who mis-heard the boy. In his chronicle he wrote, by mistake …

his son said he had a narrow escape…

**9** *As sure as eggs is eggs* – absolutely certain
This probably has nothing to with eggs, hens or chickens – and that's no yolk, all white? In the 17th century mathematicians were experimenting with *algebra*. They were finding the value of '$x$' and '$y$' and so on. Lots of things could vary, but one thing was certain … you could be 'sure that '$x$' is '$x$''.

**10** *As bald as a coot* – completely hairless
A coot is a bird. And, surprise, surprise, it is *not* bald. It is a little black duck with a white head. This white patch is of feathers. So if you

WHY HAVE YOU TATTOED RABBITS ON YOUR HEAD, DAD?

FROM A DISTANCE THEY LOOK LIKE HARES.

call someone *bald as a coot* then you are really saying their head is covered with feathers! Some men are very sensitive about being called bald. Don't mention the word *bald* in conversation. Avoid words like 'billiard ball', 'boiled egg' and 'coot' at all costs. Simply say they have 'a high forehead' or 'a wide parting'. And *don't* forget to tell them how attractive it is!

> *Answer:* There was a word from Turkey that came into the English language in the 19th century. This word should be used to describe number 8 above. William Tell's son did not say, 'That was an arrow escape,' or even 'That was a narrow escape.' Because (a) the story is fiction and (b) he only spoke German. He probably said 'Yikes!' (in German). By the way, the Turkish word we can apply to number 8? Bosh!

## Wicked whipping words

Sometimes people can use figures of speech to play practical jokes. Here are two really nasty jokes that you would never dream of playing on your friends ... would you?

### Go for a pennyworth of salad oil

In Norman France, schoolboys were bent over a saddle and flogged. The Old French word for saddle was *salade*. The English of the Middle Ages borrowed the word *salade* to mean a flogging. *Salad oil* was a figure of speech meaning a beating with birch twigs. And pity help you if you didn't understand that figure of speech!

A particularly nasty joke on April Fool's Day was to send a child to the saddle-maker's shop for 'a pennyworth of salad oil'. The poor child would expect to get some oil to pour over their salad ... instead they'd get a beating from the saddle-maker.

Other jolly little whipping words were, *taste the end of a rope* or *a touch of the cat.* The *cat* wasn't your next-door moggy, of course, but nine leather straps called a *cat o' nine tails.* Of course you could be lucky and the room might be too small to use the cat o' nine tails – and that's where we get the figure of speech, *too small to swing a cat.*

Nowadays young workers may be sent to a hardware store and told to ask for a 'long stand'. They are kept waiting. After an hour someone says, 'What did you want?'

'A long stand.'

'Well you've just had one – an *hour-long* stand. Ho! Ho!'

*Did you know...?*

An old figure of speech was *shoot the cat.* But this had nothing to do with blasting a moggy with a pistol. It comes from the fact that cats were known for being sick – another figure of speech was 'sick as a cat' – so *shoot the cat* meant vomit. You really wanted to know that, didn't you?

59

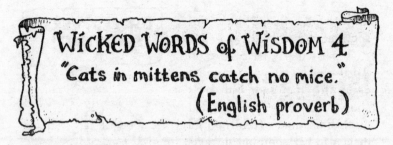

Meaning? Get your gloves off and get down to some work –
even if it is freezing in the classroom.

# Fascinating foreign languages

English borrows words from foreign languages. But they get their own back and borrow from English! Can you work out what these foreign words mean just from the sound of them?

| COUNTRY | WORD | CLUE |
|---|---|---|
| 1 FRANCE | ALLOMAN | he'll connect you! |
| 2 JAPAN | RUSHAWA | busy time in town? |
| 3 GERMANY | TWENS | teenagers go into them... |
| 4 LITHUANIA | MUVING PIKCERAS | on a silver screen? |
| 5 SPAIN | SUETER | to keep you warm? |
| 6 THE FORMER YUGOSLAVIA | PEDA | You've earned it! |
| 7 ITALY | COL CREAM | You have to face it... |
| 8 CHINA | TELEFUNG | used by French alloman! |
| 9 POLAND | AYSKRYM | Strawberry or Vanilla? |
| 10 UKRAINE | HERKOT | a barber will give you one? |

Not every country likes this 'borrowing' from English. In France there are laws against using English words in official documents when French words will do. A sarcastic French newspaper, *Le Monde*, suggested that the French need a word for 'sandwich' since they keep borrowing the English word. Maybe the French would be better asking for *deux morceaux de pain avec quelque chose au milieu* (two bits of bread with something in the middle). What a mouthful! (The words, not the sandwich you dummy!)

*Did you know...?*
Nine words appear over and over again in English writing. In fact they make up a quarter of most pieces of writing. Those nine are: *and, be, have, it, of, the, to, will, you.*

# Groovy games with wicked words

People have always enjoyed playing word games. 'I spy with my little eye' is perfect for people with a great amount of time and a small amount of brain. (Teachers enjoy playing it.) But to really enjoy words you should try something a bit more challenging. Here are a few wicked word games ...

## Daft dictionary

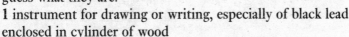

**For:** Any number of players.
**Rules:** Take a dictionary and pick a word that most people know and read out the definition – what the word means. The others have to guess the word. Here are five. Can you guess what they are?
1 instrument for drawing or writing, especially of black lead enclosed in cylinder of wood
2 enclosure for swine
3 one who absents himself from place of work and especially a child who stays away from school
4 contrary to the law
5 an Australian hardwood missile

**Alternative rules:** If you haven't got a dictionary handy you can always make up your own daft definitions. Here are the *same* clues again as they *don't* appear in the dictionary ...
1 you can drag a horse to water, but this must be lead ...
2 what a pig wears around its neck ... or the staff room
3 a real insect ... or Julie Wilton when Wimbledon tennis is on the television
4 a sick bird ... or Gary Grint's bicycle lights
5 what you say to frighten a meringue

## Fictionary Dictionary

**For:** Two teams of three.

**Rules:** Each team picks unusual words from a dictionary. They then give the opposition three possible meanings for the word, only one of which is true. The opposition try to guess the right meaning. Then it's the turn of the other team to guess.

But, are you any good? How many can you score out of the following four wacky words? (If you can't find a friend to test then try these genuine words on your teacher! Watch them scratch their heads till the splinters fly!)

1 *Topia*

**a)** an ancient Greek wig, worn by the chief magistrate to show his authority (as a judge wears a wig in court today)

**b)** an ancient Roman mural showing a landscape. Used to decorate houses. As in, 'Would you like to peer at my topia?'

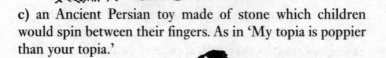

**c)** an Ancient Persian toy made of stone which children would spin between their fingers. As in 'My topia is poppier than your topia.'

**2** *Clicko*
**a)** 1920s US slang for successful – usually in the movies. As in, 'That was a clicko flic!'
**b)** a 1930s German furniture polish with a trigger that 'clicked' out squirts of the polish before the days of aerosol cans. The adverts read, 'No more sticko, we use Clicko!'

**c)** a famous performing dog in Barnum and Bailey's travelling carnival. The only dog who could count up to a million. His master's catch phrase was, 'That's not Clicko's only trick, though!'

**3** *Tiw*
**a)** World War II navy word standing for *Taking In Water* – an emergency call, like SOS but not so urgent.
**b)** an old Celtic word, now used in Wales, to describe a sneeze – just as in English we'd say Atishoo!
**c)** an Anglo–Saxon god before the Anglo–Saxons became Christian. The god gave his name to a day of the week – Tiw's-day (or Tuesday).

**4** *Netty*

**a)** a word used to describe old clothes which have worn so thin they can be seen through. As in, 'Pity my poor and netty clothes' – Shakespeare.

**b)** a word still used in the north-east of England meaning toilet. As in, 'Please, miss, can I leave the room? I need the netty.'

**c)** a Scottish word for a monster that inhabits a loch. As in, 'Ye'll get a fine netty in yer net yet, Betty pet!' **EEK!**

*Answers:* 1 b) 2 a) 3 c) 4 b)

**Score: 4** – Cheat! **3** – Clever clogs. **2** – average. **1** – average for a teacher. **0** – what the French call an *egghead* ... and that doesn't mean 'clever'!

## Knickers

**For:** Two or more players.

**Rules:** Dead simple. One player must answer every question with a single word each time ... choose a word like 'slime', 'snot', 'eyeballs' or something equally disgusting. However, if they laugh (or even give a hint of a Mona Lisa smile) they have lost.

Here's an example where the answer word is *knickers* ...

**Q:** What do you wear on your head when you go to bed?

**A:** Knickers

**Q:** What do you call your cat?

**A:** Knickers

**Q:** What do you use to strain your tea?

**A:** Knickers

**Q:** When you hand your homework to Miss Allott, you put it in her what?

**A:** You must be joking!

## Amazing anagrams

Mix up the letters of a word and spell a new word. That's an *anagram*. So *t-a-m-e* can become *meat*, *mate* or *team*.

But the cleverest anagrams are the ones where the new word means something similar to the original word (or words). For example *they see* becomes *the eyes*.

Here are eight clever anagrams you can bore your friends/family/teachers with. Say, 'Did you know…?

1 *astronomer* is an anagram of *moon starer*
2 *schoolmaster* is an anagram of *the classroom*
3 *softheartedness* is an anagram of *often sheds tears*
4 *slot machines* is an anagram of *cash lost in 'em*

5 *funeral* is an anagram of *real fun*
6 *absence makes the heart grow fonder* is an anagram of *he wants back dearest gone from here*
7 *punishment* is an anagram of *nine thumps*

8 *two plus eleven* is an anagram of *one plus twelve*.

Got the idea? Then solve these anagrams (with the help of a clue) to give two famous names …
1 HATED FOR ILL – he was hated because of what he did in the war!
2 OLD WEST ACTION – and he stars in films with plenty of that action.

Theodosia Goodman was a star of silent movies but her director needed a more dramatic name. He liked the exciting sounds of *Arab death* and scrambled the letters to come up with her new name – *Theda Bara*.

## Pangrams

If you can't manage an anagram then try a *pangram*. What has this sentence got?

*Six plump boys guzzled cheap raw vodka quite joyfully*

It is a pangram because it has all 26 letters of the alphabet in it. There are 45 letters in that sentence. Can you create a *pangram* with fewer?

## Oddbod boys

Is your name an anagram? Here are ten sentences that contain mixed-up boys' names. Can you **a)** find the boy's name then **b)** untangle it? (Are you one of them?)

1 Here comes Slime.
2 What a Clean boy.
3 He looks Ashen.
4 Evil's his name.
5 He should be Nailed.
6 Larches is very wooden.
7 The girls call him Dolly.
8 Lace is very rich.
9 Every school needs a Warden.
10 Regard that stupid boy.

A famous 20th-century British poet was called Thomas Stearns Eliot – the letters of his name proudly spell, 'To the arts I am a lesson'. (Or 'Loathsome train sets' to his mates!) But he decided he wanted to be known as T. S. Eliot ... and that's an anagram of ... 'toilets'!

Still, there are worse things than having an anagram for a name. You could have been named (as some children were) Neil Down, Luke Sharp, Ure A Pig, Safety First (who grew up to become a doctor) and Henry Will Burst.

## Magic mix-ups

Medieval magicians believed in the Power Of The Anagram. This anagram magic consisted of taking the letters of a person's name and mixing them up. The true nature of the person was then revealed.

For example, one of the courtiers of King James I took his letters, J-a-m-e-s S-t-u-a-r-t, and made ... 'a just master'.

What a creep! He *didn't* tell old James he was also 'Jesus' rat mat', 'just ate rams', 'just seam tar', 'just ate mars', 'uses jam tart' or 'sues jam tart', did he?

Did anyone look at Queen Victoria's hat and say, 'I cover antique.' Did her servant have spots and announce, 'I quit over acne!' Did old Vic ever scream at her priest, 'O! Quieten vicar!'? And she definitely never announced, 'I acquire one TV.' They are all anagrams of Queen Victoria.

Elizabeth the First was a terror. Would you dare tell her that her anagram suggests she is a bighead? 'Her hat size fit belt'? Or would you comment on her black and white teeth ... 'zebra teeth is filth'.

Who would tell Oliver Cromwell he's a 'more evil WC roll'? You may prefer to tell Margaret Thatcher she was 'that great charmer'? No?

What terrible secret is hidden in your name?

*Did you know…?*
One of the oddest pieces of graffiti was found in 1805. An American expedition set off to explore and map the west. Very few Europeans had been there before the Lewis and Clark expedition, but Jonathan Bowman was one of them. And he left his name to prove it. Lewis and Clark found Bowman's name … tattooed on the leg of a Native American woman!

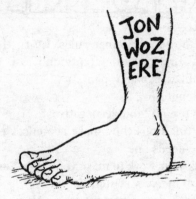

# Gruesome grammar

Languages have rules. These rules are called *grammar*. You know the sort of thing …

## Rotten rules

Here are the top ten grammar rules. Learn these. Impress your teachers, amaze your parents and lose your friends. (Well, no one likes a smarty-pants!)

1 Don't spel rongly.

2 Don't never use no 'double-negatives'.

3 Always use full stops they make sentences easier to read every sentence needs one

4 Always check your work to make you haven't any words out.

5 Always a verb in every sentence.

6 Always, word order important is, reading easier to make, remember.

7 Don't use a comma, where you don't need, one.

8 Don't use attenuated asseverations when uncomplicated vocabulary will suffice.

9 Alway's use apostrophe's as your teacher's tell you.

10 And *never* start a sentence with … 'and'!

But don't worry too much. If your teacher picks on you for poor grammar, just tell him or her that even American Presidents have bad grammar. Then quote this masterpiece from the former US President, George Bush:

# Hocus pocus

Want to turn your deadliest enemy into a frog? Or, worse, a prince? Or, worst of all, a teacher? Then you need wicked wishing words like *hocus pocus*.

There are two explanations for how *hocus pocus* came to be used by magicians.

1 It comes from the name of an old Norse god, Ochus Bocus.

2 It comes from the Latin words used in the Roman Catholic church service. It is a short form of *hoc est corpus meum* – 'this is my body'.

But *hocus pocus* is just one wicked wish that has been used over the centuries. Here are some other wicked wishing words ...

### Abracadabra

A lucky word in the Middle Ages was *Abracadabra*. This was said to be a charm made from the Hebrew initials of the Father, the Son and the Holy Spirit. The word was written on paper and hung from the neck by a linen thread for luck. If you want to try it then it must be written like this ...

## Powerful words

*Agla* Got a poltergeist in the pantry or a spook in the spare room? Get rid of it with the word *agla*. It is an abbreviation of the Hebrew words meaning, 'Thou art forever mighty, Lord.'

*Ananisapta* Got a spot on your nose? Wish it away with *ananisapta*. No, that's not a new type of antiseptic cream – it's a powerful word. Write it on a parchment and wear it round your neck. Like *abracadabra* it will protect you from disease ... well, maybe if you're *very* lucky!

*Hola Nola Massa* To protect you from evils (like homework, housework or boys who pick their noses), recite these words from the Middle Ages ...

*Ofano, Oblamo, Ospergo.*
*Pax Sax Sarax.*
*Afa Afca Nostra.*
*Cerum, Heaium, Lada Frium.*

*Y ran qui ran* Worried about catching rabies after being bitten by a mad dog? Worry no more. Here is a cure ... simply write these wishing words on a piece of paper: *y ran qui ran, casram casratem casratosque.* Place it in an eggshell and force it down your throat. Actually, if I were you, I'd run to the nearest hospital.

*Pyrzqxgl* Tired of your ugly body? Want a change? Or tired of teacher's ugly mush and want to be taught by someone with film-star looks? Say the word *pyrzqxgl* and your wish will come true. Just two small catches.

**1** You have to pronounce it properly.

**2** This was invented by L. Frank Baum and used in his book, *The Magic of Oz*. Don't get too excited by the possibilities, you will probably be disappointed. So, remember

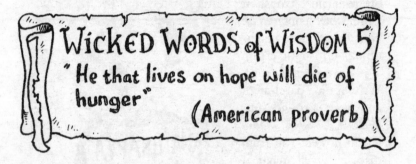

WICKED WORDS of WISDOM 5
"He that lives on hope will die of hunger"
(American proverb)

And so will he or she who lives on fresh air.

# Ice-cool invaders

## History of the language – part 2

1 The Anglo-Saxons were settling nicely into the old Celtic ground when in AD 787 they were challenged by a team from Scandinavia playing as the Vikings.

2 In a tough match the Vikings soon scored and looked like winning.

3 Then the English brought on a new striker, Alfred the Great, and turned the game around.

**4** Many Vikings stayed in the north and left their language, especially in place names ...

The Vikings scattered a few of their words around the country but mainly in the north and east where they had settled. They gave the north and the east many place names ...

- *by* meant 'farm' or 'town' so there were Vikings in Derby, Grimsby and Rugby – if you live there you might spot the odd Viking chasing polar bears.
- *Thorp* meant 'village' – so they settled in Althorpe, Mablethorpe and Scunthorpe.
- *Thwaite* was their name for a lonely spot – like Braithwaite and Langthwaite.
- *Toft* was Viking-speak for a piece of ground – Lowestoft and Nortoft.

The Vikings also gave us some surnames. Often the names ending *son*. So, if you are a Davison living in Derby or a Ronson in Rugby or a Lawson in Lowestoft you could have Viking blood running through your veins. (But *don't look now* because **a)** you will make red stains all over this book and **b)** Viking blood is the same colour as other blood and it does not have 'Viking' written in the middle of it like a stick of Blackpool Rock.)

Thanks to the Viking language you can now have the following conversation with your loved one...

YOUR **FLAT FRECKLED FACE** MAKES ME **GASP AWKWARDLY**, LIKE A **FELLOW** WITH AN **EGG** IN HIS **MOUTH**. LET ME **CALL** YOU, MY **DAZZLING, GLITTERING KID** OR I'LL **DIE MEEKLY** IN THE **DIRT** LIKE A **REINDEER!**

**GET** LOST, YOU **ROTTEN SCAB**, BEFORE I STICK THIS **STEAK KNIFE** IN YOUR **SCOWLING, MUCKY, DIRTY FACE**. YOUR **LEGS** WOULD **SCARE** A **SCORE** OF **BULLS**, SO **CRAWL** OUT OF A **LOW WINDOW!**

See? How on earth would you manage without those magical words?

# Interesting initials

Cut a word short and you have an *abbreviation*. Once people rode on an omnibus ... now they simply take the abbreviation – the bus.

Call something (or someone) by their *initials* and you have an abbreviation. Ever played a CD (Compact Disc)? Then you've played an abbreviation.

But many modern abbreviations have the letters chosen so they make a new word – it's easier to remember that way. These are called *acronyms*.

• The Association of Traders in Souvenirs and Novelties sold toys. So they arranged their name into Souvenir And Novelty Trade Association (SANTA).

WELCOME TO THIS EMERGENCY MEETING OF THE BRITISH UNION OF RADISH PRODUCERS. FIRST ITEM ON THE AGENDA: WE NEED TO FIND A NEW ACRONYM...

• A group calling themselves Mothers Against Drunk Driving (MADD) was formed. Unfortunately this gave their enemies a chance to form Drivers Against Madd Mothers (DAMM)!

• A Swedish pop group had two men, Benny and Bjorn, and two women, Agnetha and Annifrid. Initials BBAA? No. AABB? No. BAAB? Got it! ABBA!

- Some acronyms come into the language and we forget they are the initials of something else. Take the word POSH. It's come to mean 'snobbish, high class'. But the story goes that it comes from the days of British people travelling to India and the east. The rich chose to travel on the port (left) side going out to India and the starboard (right) side coming home – because they were the sides shaded from the burning sun. So the rich were Port Out, Starboard Home ... POSH.

- Not every acronym catches on but BICYEA ice cream was a success in America – it claimed to be the Best Ice Cream You Ever Ate.
- Dot-dot-dot, dash-dash-dash, dot-dot-dot spells SOS in Morse code. Seamen agreed to use it because it is easy to remember. Later, people claimed it was an abbreviation

and stood for *Save Our Souls*. It *doesn't* stand for that any more than it stands for Sick Of Sausages, Stupid Old School or Shove Off Stanley.

- World War II (WWII) saw hundreds of new acronyms created by the WD (War Department) and the army. Acronym mania didn't getting any better in the nineties! Now we have computer acronyms to worry about. I *could* tell you my PC has a CD-ROM drive and a WP with WYSIWYG display attached to a LASER printer with LCD panel and Wi-Fi – you'd possibly be impressed, probably be confused, so what's the point? The Editor of the *New York Times* hated acronyms ... so he created one! APPALLING – Acronym production, particularly at lavish level, is no good.

Sometimes an acronym is only understood by an expert. When they use that acronym (or any other special word) to confuse normal people like you and me then we can accuse them of using 'jargon'.

# Jolly jargon

Some people have their own words for their own concerns. It's not a problem … unless they use it when they're talking to people who haven't a clue what they mean.

Or unless you use it to show off …

## Say it again

*Dear Mrs Barnes,*
*Thank you for your recent letter. You asked for a bus shelter at Ligett Lane. Unfortunately, because of government spending cuts we have been ordered to reduce the building of bus shelters. There may be more money next year for new shelters but shelters already on the waiting list will be built first.*

Got that? 'Thanks for asking for a bus shelter. Sorry, we can't afford it at present.' Unfortunately, that is *not* the letter Mrs Barnes received. Someone in West Yorkshire Council used *jargon* to come up with this wicked collection of words – it means the same, but it you'll not believe how difficult that simple message becomes …

*Dear Mrs Barnes,*
*I refer to your recent letter in which you submit a request for the provision of a bus passenger shelter in Ligett Lane at the inward stopping place for service 31 adjacent to Gledhow Primary School. The stated requirement for a bus shelter at this location has been noted but as you may be aware shelter erection at all locations within West Yorkshire has been constrained in recent times as a result of instructions issued by the West Yorkshire Metropolitan County Council in the light of the government's cuts in public expenditure and, although it seems likely that the capital budget for shelter provision will be enhanced in the forthcoming financial year, it is axiomatic that residual requests in respect of prospective shelter sites identified as having priority, notably those named in earlier programmes of shelter erection, will take precedence in any future shelter programme.*

That's jargon!

*Did you know…?*

One of the rarest languages was Ubykh. Once 50,000 people in the Crimea spoke it. By 1984 only one man still spoke it … and he was 80 years old. He died in 1992, taking the language with him.

## Severely sick sick-notes

Jargon has its uses. Learn a few wicked words and baffle your teachers. Next time you fancy a term off school then write a note with some complicated medical terms in it. Your teacher will be so busy rushing for the medical dictionary that he or she will fail to notice something very important … *the letter is in your handwriting.* It's a *forgery!* Try this for starters …

Dear Sir

Sorry Paul/Paula/Ratface is absent from school. He/she/it has been to see a ~~barai~~ bariatrics specialist who used an auriscope to examine his circumorbital haemotoma. This was the result of my son/daughter/gerbil walking into a door which almost left him/her/it edentulous. Since the accident the surbated eye requires zomotherapy so he/she/it can pass the optotype test. Once the carphology has stopped my child should return to school within a year.

Yours Otorhinolaringologically, My MuM

You'd better be familiar with the meanings, just in case the school attendance officer calls.

| | |
|---|---|
| a bariatrics specialist | doctor who specializes in fatness |
| auriscope | one of those little magnifying lenses with a light attached |
| circumorbital haematoma | a black eye |
| edentulous | toothless |
| surbated | bruised |
| zomotherapy | placing raw meat on an injury to help cure it |
| optotype | a chart with letters on, used by opticians to test eyesight |
| carphology | the bad habit of picking at your bedclothes |
| otorhinolaryngologically | from the ear, nose and throat |

## Computerised claptrap

Back in 1995, when computers were still relatively new, a computer magazine offered 'a PC with 486 DX 25 MHz performance, 8 Kb cache and integral co-processor up to 20 Mb RAM, 85 Mb Hard Disk, PCMIA connectivity and fast Local Bus Video Graphics', not to mention 'Enhanced parallel, Serial Mouse, VGA, Flexconnect Interfaces, NiMH Battery and pre-loaded MS-DOS 6.0'. It then says 'Instruction manuals not included'. This is a pity. Without the manuals you probably won't even understand the advert! You may also misunderstand some of the terms ...

But don't worry. Thirty years ago no one knew what a smartphone was!

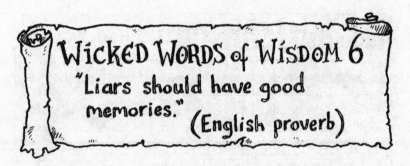

WICKED WORDS of WISDOM 6
"Liars should have good memories." (English proverb)

Meaning ... when you return to school after skiving for a day, remember what you were supposed to be ill with!

# Jesting Johnson

Dr Samuel Johnson was a fat, ugly and very untidy slob. He was an offensive man and insulted everyone … but especially women. He also gained everlasting fame for writing the first really important dictionary of the English language. (This just goes to show there could be hope for your teacher yet.) Johnson's dictionary was published in 1755 after nine years of work with the aid of six assistants.

## The Doctor's dictionary

1 The Dictionary was a serious work, but Johnson couldn't resist the odd joke. He was able to get in the odd nasty remark about people he disliked … the Scottish people for example. Johnson wrote a definition of Oats as follows …

**Oats:** A grain which is generally given to horses, but in Scotland supports the people

The Scots got their own back when they said, 'This explains why England has the most beautiful horses – but Scotland has the most beautiful women!'
2 Johnson wasn't going to be beaten. A Scotsman once argued that Scotland has many beautiful sights. Johnson agreed! 'And the most beautiful sight a Scotsman can see is the road that will lead him to England!'

SO THERE!

3 Doctor Johnson hated 'baby-talk' – like when your mum embarrasses the heck out of you by calling you in from a friendly game of alligator-wrestling with the call, 'Beansie-weensies on the table my little petal-pops'. One day Johnson saw a poor woman struggling through the rain with a baby wrapped in a shawl. He stopped the coach and offered her a lift. 'But no baby talk to that infant,' he warned. 'Or else!'

The woman sat quietly. The baby slept. Then the baby woke up and started to cry. 'Is my little dearie going to open his eyesie-piesies, then?' she asked.

'No, but I am going to open the coach door!' Johnson roared. He stopped the coach and threw her out.

4 Printing the dictionary cost money. Lots of money that Doctor Johnson didn't have. Rich people gave him gifts – in return they expected to see their names printed at the beginning of the book.

A bookseller's assistant brought a large sum to Johnson one day. The doctor stuffed it in his pocket. 'Aren't you going to make a note of who paid the money?' the boy gasped.

'No,' Johnson snapped.

'How can you print a list of the people who gave money?'

'I can't,' Johnson shrugged. 'Firstly because I've lost the names of the people who paid ... and second because I've spent all the money.'

5 A cheeky young man once met Doctor Johnson at a party. 'I say, Johnson,' he said. 'I bet you wish you were as young and fit as me.'

Johnson looked at him. 'Not if it meant being as stupid as you,' he sniffed.

*Did you know...?*

Noah Webster caused a fuss with his first American Dictionary too by changing some spellings. But the third edition of 1961 caused a lot of trouble when it said *ain't* was a perfectly good word, and so was *piss-poor*! (A bishop objected to that one.)

# Knock-knock

Knock! Knock!
Who's there?
Language expert.
Language expert who?
Language expert who can tell you why you spell the work 'k-nock' but say it 'nock'.
I never asked.
But I'm going to tell you anyway. The reason it is spelled k–nock (like k–night and k–nee) is that this is the way the English said these words in the Middle Ages. Over the years the 'k' was dropped when people spoke it ... but left in the spelling.
Yawn ... thank you!
My pleasure.

Knock-Knock jokes have been popular for over 50 years. They began with a simple twist of a name ...

Knock! Knock!
Who's there?
Arthur.
Arthur who?
Arfa pound of tuppenny rice, arf a pound of treacle ...

But in time people didn't care what word answered the knock. It didn't have to be a name ...

Knock! Knock!
Who's there?
Wooden shoe.
Wooden shoe who?
Wooden shoe like to know?

Or the trick would be to end the riddle unexpectedly ...

Knock! Knock!
Who's there?
You.
You who?
You-hoo! nice to see you!

It is possible to play Knock-Knock as a word game. Two people (or two teams) pick words that have been put into a hat. They have to make that word line three of the riddle and come up with a suitable line five. Try it with these words ...

1 *Police*
2 *Howard*
3 *Madam*
4 *Ivor*
5 *Freeze*

Can you do it? Here are the answers (for the real dummies who can't):

1 *P-lease let me in because I'm cold*
2 *How-would you like a punch in the knee-cap?*
3 *Ma-damn finger's caught in the door.*
4 *I've-a bit of trouble reaching the door bell.*
5 *For-he's a jolly good fellow.*

Can you do something with your own name?

# Lousy Latin

The Romans ruled England but they didn't mix with the British peasants so much. After 400 years the Romans went back to Rome but didn't leave too many words behind.

Missionaries came from Rome around AD 500 but only left a few hundred words. Then, 1,000 years later, British writers in the Middle Ages began using Latin again so they could write to people in other countries. Latin was a 'common' language. Latin words didn't replace English words but went alongside them.

Peasants (like you and me) used English for speaking; writers used French; *really* clever people used Latin.

So, if you want to impress your head teacher and win the school prize for being 'Brain of the Year' then try throwing in a few Latin words …

# Muddled Mrs Malaprop

Mrs *Who?* No. Mrs *Malaprop*. She was a character in a play by a writer called Richard Brinsley Sheridan. The play was called *The Rivals* ... and when it was first produced it was an instant flop. But brave Brinsley rewrote it and ten days later it was a huge success!

What has this got to do with Mrs Malaprop? I hear you asking. I'm coming to that. Mrs Malaprop was a character in the play. A pompous, ignorant woman who liked to use big words ... but kept getting them wrong. For example ...

FOR HEAVEN'S SAKE TELL US WHAT IS THE MATTER?

WHY, MURDER'S THE MATTER! SLAUGHTER'S THE MATTER! KILLING'S THE MATTER! BUT HE CAN GIVE YOU THE PERPENDICULARS...

Wise wordsters will know that she really meant *particulars* (the details) not *perpendiculars* (the uprights).

Ever since *The Rivals* was performed, the wrong use of a word has been known as a *malapropism*.

Richard B. Sheridan didn't *invent* malapropisms, you

understand. Writers of comedy plays (including Shakespeare) had been using them for years. But Mrs Malaprop became the most famous character to use them.

Even with modern education people still use the wrong words. And when they do it is still funny – especially if, like Mrs Malaprop, they think they are a little bit more important than the rest of us. Parents do it ...

Teachers do it ...

History is horrible for it ...

Geography has a world of examples ...

English essays are full of them …

Science pupils have problems with them …

Religious Education is riddled with them …

Educated people do it …

These are all actual examples. Needles to say, you or I wouldn't do it. We are far too inelegant.

# Nasty Normans

## History of the language – part 3

1 In 1066 the new England manager, Harold, beat a weak Viking team at Stamford Bridge (Yorkshire, not Chelsea).

2 But before his squad had a chance of a breather, the Normans from France attacked Harold's empty goal at the other end of the pitch – Hastings.

3 The Normans won a famous away victory and team-boss William took over the English ground.

**4** The Normans passed new laws and ran the ground in French. But the Old English language survived among the ordinary supporters.

In fact the Old English changed to something we call Middle English. And the power of the word was still in the hands of the people who could write.

Just 70 years after William the Conqueror's invasion, the monks were brave enough to write nasty things about the Norman King Stephen. He probably wasn't as bad as all that … but the monks didn't like him so they gave him a bad report in their Peterborough Chronicle. They said nasty things (in English, of course) like …

> *I ne can ne I ne mai tellen alle the wunder ne alle the pines that he did wrecce men on his land and that lasted xix intre wile Stephne was king.*

What do you mean, you don't understand it? It's English, isn't it? Oh, very well. Here it is a bit updated …

> *I know not, nor I may not tell, all the trouble nor all the pain that he did wreak (on) men on his land, and that lasted 19 winters while Stephen was king.*

See? Not so difficult after *alle* … I mean *all*. The report went on (and I'll let you have it in modern English to save your brain cells) …

*Always it became worse and worse. When the poor people had no more to give then he robbed and burned all the villages. Wretched people died of hunger, some who were rich men had to beg to stay alive, some fled from the country. There was never a more miserable time in this country, not even when we were ruled by savages. Against all the old laws they did not spare the churches or the churchyards but seized all the wealth that was there before burning the church and everything else. They did not spare the priest's land or the bishop's but robbed the monks and clergy and anyone else who had power.*

Look at that last sentence again. Maybe you can spot what lay behind the monks' hatred of Stephen? Unfortunately we don't have Stephen's side of the story.

IT'S SO UNFAIR! I DIDN'T BURN ANY CHURCHES! I JUST SINGED THEM A BIT!

Of course the Normans spoke French and the English spoke English, but the two languages did begin to affect one another. The Normans may have won the war and they may have ruled the land – but English won the language battle! Just 111 years after the Battle of Hastings (in the year 1177 in case you can't add up) a man called Saccharin wrote ...

> *Now that the English and the Norman people have been living together and marrying, the two nations have become so mixed that it is scarcely possible today to tell who is English and who is Norman.*

But the Normans did have *some* effect. If you wonder why we use *qu* when we could use the sensible *kw*, blame the Normans. Everyone in England was happily spelling words like *kwene*. (This made perfect sense because she was usually married to a *king*.) Then along came the Normans in 1066, and decided they liked it better spelled *queen*.

(If the Normans hadn't done this then the English might

have laughed at someone who called himself William the Conkeror! It's very hard to conker a people who laugh at you.)

*Did you know...?*
William the Conqueror tried to learn English ... but failed!

## Middle English – history of the language – part 4

Middle English came between Old English and Modern English. It came in the *Middle*. That's why it is called *Middle* English. Get it? Of course it wasn't called *Middle* English in those days. People probably thought they were using slap-bang-modern up-to-date English back then.

One day someone will call *your* English 'Late Middle English' or something. But by then you'll be so long gone that you won't be too offended.

The Norman French words had crept into English by now. Thanks to the Normans you can now use words the Old English didn't have. Words like …

# Odd onomatopoeia

Say, 'On a mat a pier.' See? Simple! All it means is a word that sounds like the thing it describes. So, a snake goes 'sssss!'. The first person to be hissed at by a snake might have run back to his family and warned, 'Ssss-nik! Ssss-nik!' and the name stuck. 'Ssss-nik!' became snake. Well, maybe.

'Cuckoo' describes the sound of the bird and 'crack' is the noise of breaking. Clever professors think that's how most of our words started. Other clever professors disagree!

All we need to know is that words don't just *mean* something. They have *sound* too. And the wickedest word speakers and writers can use those sounds. So can you.

The *sl* sound is usually used for unpleasant things. Insult your deadliest enemy with a collection of sl words …

YOU'RE A SLY SLOUCH; A SLOVENLY SLAVE WHO EATS SLOPS WITH A SLOBBERY SLURP AND LIVES IN A SLEAZY SLUM WITH SLIMY SLUGS!

I SHOULD SLAP YOU FOR SLANDER!

**Onomatopoeic joke**
Q: What goes 'clip'?
A: A one-legged horse.

# Potty proverbs

A proverb is a popular saying, usually with a piece of useful advice. It's the wisdom of hundreds of years concentrated into a few, well-chosen words. The wickedest of words, in fact. Such as, 'Absence makes the heart grow fonder' – if your loved one leaves then you'll miss them terribly.

Or, 'Out of sight, out of mind' – if your loved one leaves then you won't miss them at all. (You will gather from this that not all proverbs are as clever as they try to make out.) But sometimes a proverb is so wickedly brilliant that you wonder why you never thought of it yourself. Where would we be without these gems ...

1 *Boys will be boys.* (Amazing! Just when you thought that boys will be ten-ton turkeys in top hats.)
2 *Dead men tell no tales.* (How very true. And fried eggs tell no lies.)
3 *What will be will be.* (What will be will be *what?* You may well ask. What will be will be ... in the future?)
4 *Never say die.* (Polite people say, 'push up daisies', 'count worms', or 'hand in the dinner pail', but they *never* say *die*.)

**5** *Forgive and forget.* (How wise. Yet these few, well-chosen, concentrated words could be concentrated even further! This proverb should really just say *Forget*. Because, if you *forget* you don't have to forgive, because you've forgotten what it was you had to forgive. See?)

## Don't count your chickens before they hatch

Proverbs are ancient wisdom and you *should not make fun of them.* Yet some people actually take proverbs and turn them into *jokes.* This is quite shameful and not the sort of thing you will find in a respectable book like this. So, I shall *not* tell you the story of the Count of Kent County – whose name was Carl …

I shall not tell you that the Count of Kent County was a very rich man. Very, very, very rich. Alas, he was also very mean.

King Henry of Hampden Hall needed money so he decided to tax Count Carl of Kent County.

'I want your money, Kent Count of Count Carly!' he demanded. (I should point out he had a habit of muddling his words.)

'I've hidden it King Hall of Hampden Henry,' the Kent County Count called. (You'll notice he mixed up his words too.)

'Then I'll have to cut off your head! Carl Count of Count Kenty!' King Henry hissed.

The King's men grabbed poor Carl and carted him off to a chopping block. 'Tell me!' the King said.

'Never!' the quivering Carl countered.

'Cut Count Kent of Carl County's cackle!' the king cried.

The executioner swung the axe. It began to fall when Count Carl screamed, 'I'll tell you! The money's hidden in the …'

CHOP! Went the axe.

SCHLOPP! Went the neck.

PLOP! Went the head on the floor.

'STOP!' Went King Henry.

'Ooops!' went the executioner. 'Sorry, boss. Too late.'

King Henry tore Count Carl of Kent County's castle apart – but he never found that treasure.

'Just goes to show,' the king (who muddled his words) would sigh. 'Never hatchet your counts before they chicken.'

## Pick a proverb

Until the 1960s, children were expected to learn proverbs by heart. Since 'words cut more than swords,' here are a few to help you impress your teacher, (with some helpful explanations).

*Did you know...?*
A proverb says 'Two's company, three's a crowd.' But what are four and five? Answer: Nine!

## Proverbs game

**For:** Two or more players.
**Rules:**
1 The 'guesser' leaves the room.
2 The group choose a proverb.
3 The guesser returns and asks the group questions, one at a time – any question, from 'What did you do on holiday?' to 'What did Jack and Jill climb up?'
4 The first answer contains the first word of the proverb, the second answer contains the second word, etc.
5 After the last word has been given, the guesser can guess the whole proverb.

**Example:**
Proverb is: 'Red sky at night, shepherds' delight.'
Question 1 may be: 'What colour fruit grows on apple trees?'
Answer 1 may be: 'Red apples or green ones depending on what sort of apple tree it is.'
But ... beware! The children's author, A.A. Milne, described a game of Proverbs that didn't quite go to plan.

The group sent William out of the room and started to talk about the proverb they should use. They didn't want to make it too easy. After a lot of arguing they came up with the ancient Persian proverb, 'A wise man is kind to his dog, but a poor man riseth early in the morning.'

Someone went to the door to call William in to start guessing. But absent-minded William had grown bored, forgotten why he was in the hallway ... and gone to bed!

## Impressive proverbs

Want to impress your teachers? Want to amaze your parents? Want to cheat at the Proverbs game and come up with something no one has heard of? Then learn one or two of these genuine (but wickedly wacky) proverbs from around the world. (You might not understand them, but they sound *incredibly* wise.)

1 A teacher is better than two books. (German)

112

**2** The wise man sits on the hole in his carpet. (Persian)

**3** A bald head is soon shaved. (Irish)

**4** Many a man's tongue has broken his nose. (English)

**5** A man with a head of wax should not walk in the sun. (Latin)

**6** Tomorrow is often the busiest day of the week. (Spanish)

**7** It does not always rain when the pig squeals. (American)

**8** Never go to the devil with a dish cloth in your hand. (Scottish)

**9** When the mouse laughs at the cat there is a hole near by. (Nigerian)

**10** In the kingdom of hope there is no winter. (Russian)

# Quaint qabbalah

Never get behind the 17th letter of the alphabet because it's always a 'Q'. (Queue – get it?)

*When you write the letter Q*
*Always follow with a U?*
*That old rule is wrong by far …*
*Ask the people of Qatar!*

And look at words like *qabbalah*. Especially because *qabbalah* is one of those words about words. In the Middle Ages the *qabbalah* was a set of mystic practices – a bit like looking at your horoscope in the newspaper today. Followers of the *qabbalah* believed quite simply that *words* were magical in themselves. They were a code sent by God. All you had to do was to understand their secret and you would understand the meaning of life.

How did this work? Give each letter a number: A = 1, B = 2 and so on till Z = 26. Now, add up the value of the letters in a word. B-E-D is 2 + 5 + 4. So, BED is 11.

Now take some important words or names in your life and see which ones come to the same total (give or take one or two). If they match then there is a magical connection. Here are some examples …

1 KING + CHAIR = THRONE (so kings are meant to sit on thrones)

2 BOOK + LOAN = LIBRARY (so books are made to be borrowed from libraries)

3 KEEP + OFF = GRASS (so grass wasn't meant to be walked on.)

Incredible isn't it? Now take my name – TERRY. That's an 86. SUNDAY is an 84 and, would you believe it? I was born on a Sunday!! (Of course I was christened TERENCE, which is 70, and that's *nearly* the 72 of MONDAY. Astonishingly I was *not* born on a Monday … but I did once break my leg on a Saturday. Unbelievable!)

Imagine running your life by looking at your numbers before you got out of bed! Aren't you glad you don't live in the Middle Ages … because here are two more sets of 'magic' numbers to help you decide whether to believe all this.

1 MIDDLE AGES (79) = RUBBISH (79)
2 QABBALAH (42) = HO! HO! (42)

## Abraxas

The word *abraxas* is supposed to have magical powers. Through a number code (similar to the qabbalah) the letters of *abraxas* add up to 365 – the number of days in a year. You should carve these letters on a stone to make a powerful lucky charm. (Don't ask me what you do in a leap year!)

**115**

## Numberwords game

The qabbalah idea of words and numbers can be turned into a game.

**For:** You need two or more players, a pen, paper and a timer.

**Rules:** Someone picks a number ... say 81 ... and each player has to write down as many words as possible that add up to 81. Put a time limit of 5 to 10 minutes on it.

# Rotten riddles

What is red and white? Answer: pink. Questions like this are known as riddles. Riddles are one of the oldest word games. (Jokes are older than words. Cave dwellers cracked up with laughter if somebody slipped on a squashed slug or sat on a smouldering stick and burned their bum.)

Once words were used, you can be sure jokes weren't far behind.

But there are riddles in history too ...

## Greek groaners

The Ancient Greeks knew all about riddles. One of the most famous concerns a king called Oedipus who solved the riddle asked by a creature called the Sphinx ... *What has one voice, walks on four legs in the morning, on two legs at noon and on three legs in the evening?*

The answer was a *man* ... as a baby, an adult and an old person with a stick!

The Sphinx was so upset when Oedipus guessed the answer that she threw herself off a rock and into the sea. (Who said, 'Words can never hurt me'?)

## Biblical blockbusters

The Bible has riddles but they are more complicated than the Greek ones. In fact you probably wouldn't get the answer to one if you lived for threescore years and ten and had a very sick mind! One of the riddles was ...

*Out of the eater came something to eat;*
*Out of the strong came something sweet.*

Samson asked the Philistine guests this riddle and promised rich gifts if they could answer in seven days. And they *did* it! But they cheated. Samson's wife (the rotten sneak) told them the answer. The answer? A swarm of bees making honey in the corpse of a lion. (Warned you it was sick!)

## Suffering Saxons

Some people took words very seriously indeed! The Romans had riddle competitions while the Saxons and Danes even went into battle with them and used them rather like weapons. At the Battle of Maldon in AD 991 the two enemy sides exchanged insults with one another.

## English idiocies

The oldest English language riddles can be found in *The Exeter Book* written around the eighth century. On the long winter nights, when the wind moaned through the cracks in the wattle walls, families gathered round the fire and tried to outwit each other with riddles. Here is a riddle from *The Exeter Book* ...

Often I go to war with the waves and fight against the wind. I fight against both of them when I'm buried by the foam and go to seek the earth. My homeland is foreign to me. If I stay still then I am mighty in the battle. If I flee from their pulling then I have failed. They want to carry off the thing that I keep safe. I defeat them if my tail holds strong and if the stones of the earth hold me up firmly.

What is my name?

Got it? The answer is *an anchor*.

## Medieval mirth-makers

From the Middle Ages, monarchs employed jesters to entertain them with riddles. Henry VIII had jester Will Sommers to cheer him up ... but a lot of Will's jokes were a bit rude. Many were collected in a 1511 book by a man with the improbable name of Wynkyn de Worde.

119

No doubt you'll want to hear some of these wonders of wit and wisdom. Try these on a friend ...

Can you ever stop laughing at these sparkling gems? (Did you ever start?) It should be pointed out, no monarch ever died laughing. Now you know why.

## Rude rhymes

The author of the book, *Gulliver's Travels*, was a man called Swift. Occasionally, he tried making up rhymes. This one is pretty disgusting. Do *not* recite this to teacher or you will risk a kick up the answer ...

*Because I am by nature blind,*
*I wisely choose to walk behind;*
*However, to avoid disgrace,*
*I let no creature see my face.*
*My words are few, but spoke with sense;*
*And yet my speaking gives offence;*
*Or, if to whisper I presume,*
*The company will fly the room*

**Answer:** Swift politely called it a *posterior*. You may have another name for it.

## Vitty Victorians

Riddles were popular in Victorian times … even with Queen Victoria. Someone sent a riddle to Victoria and said it came from the Bishop of Salisbury. Vic and husband Albert spent three days trying to work out the answer to the riddle. In the end they got in touch with the Bishop and said, 'Tell us the answer to the riddle you sent us!'

The bishop replied, 'Riddle? I didn't send you that riddle – and I'm sorry. I don't know the answer either!'

In fact the riddle had no answer. Victoria, it was recorded, was *very angry*.

Many riddle books were published in Victorian times. A popular type of riddle was, 'What's the difference between …' You must know quite a few.
The Victorians had …

Over the years riddles grew into jokes.

(The joke is that you are expected to think of 'Elephant' as the obvious answer.)

Riddles are not as popular as they used to be and people now have fun with 'anti-riddles' … where the joke is that there is no joke.

## Modern moans

Some riddles are fun when you know the answer and watch someone scratch their head till they get splinters in their fingers. This one baffled almost the entire staff of one school – only the PE teacher got the answer! Try it on your teachers …

Billy Black's mother has three children:

1p = Penny
5p = Bob
10p = ?

What is the name of Mrs Black's third child? (Note: 5p used to be a shilling in old money and the nickname for a shilling was a 'Bob'. Just trying to be helpful.)

*Answer:* Billy of course.

Before you fall off your chair laughing, remember …

WICKED WORDS of WISDOM 7
"He who laughs last laughs longest"
(English proverb)

# Renaissance

## History of the language – part 5

No, 'Renaissance' is not another word for a type of word. It's a *time*. It began in Italy. In Britain it lasted roughly from when William Caxton brought the printing press to Britain in 1476 until about 1650.

The Renaissance was a time of new learning. And if people were learning new things (in medicine and other sciences) then they needed new words to describe them. But where do you find a new word?

Renaissance explorers discovered America and a few new foods too. There was a useful food that you could boil, fry, roast, mash or cook in its skin. What would you call it? 'That useful new vegetable' is a bit of a mouthful.

The Native American people called it *batata* – the Spanish explorers pinched that name and called it *patata*.

Renaissance scientists often went back to the dead Latin and Greek languages to borrow words …

YOU HAVE A VIRUS IN YOUR GLOTTIS THAT NECESSITATES A CAPSULE TO DISABLE IT BEFORE YOUR LARYNX IS INFECTED AND YOU DEVELOP PNEUMONIA.

BUT I ONLY HAD A SORE THROAT WHEN I CAME IN HERE!

… or they borrowed words from other foreign languages. Where did Renaissance people get these words from? Can you match the word to the country?

| Word | Country |
|------|---------|
| 1 giraffe | a) Holland |
| 2 chocolate | b) Persia |
| 3 coffee | c) France |
| 4 yacht | d) Spain |
| 5 bazaar | e) Italy |
| 6 alligator | f) Turkey |

*Answers:* 1 e) 2 c) though it originally came from an Aztec word 3 f) 4 a) 5 b) 6 d)

125

Now you can say, 'I was having coffee on my yacht that I bought at a bazaar when along came an alligator and swallowed my chocolate giraffe.'

Of course really clever Renaissance people didn't need to borrow words from anybody. They just made them up. And the greatest English maker-upper was a scribbler from Stratford called …

# Superstar Shakespeare

William Shakespeare wrote poems and plays from about 1590 till 1616 ... then he stopped because he died and that made it a bit difficult.

Will used 17,677 different words in his writing ... someone, with nothing better to do, counted them! But the wordily wicked thing is this – about 1,705 of those were new words! (And the same someone counted those too! Wicked? Or wacky?) Before brainy Bill caressed his quill you couldn't have said ...

The other odd thing (that teachers will bore you with) is that he wrote most of his plays in a sort of poetry that didn't usually rhyme – but it did have a regular *rhythm* that went

So, in Shakespeare's famous play *Romeo and Juliet*, for example, Romeo recites:

*Ah she doth teach the torches to burn bright.*

But people didn't pay their pennies to learn a bunch of new words or hear a bunch of actors go, 'di-dahh, di-dahh, di-dahh, di-dahh, di-dahh.' No. They went along to see the characters murder each other, shed buckets of stage-blood and even *eat* each other!

Shakespeare's bloodiest play of all was *Macbeth*. Here's a short extract to show how brilliant – and how totally tasteless – Will Shakespeare could be. Warning: this play contains scenes of violence that some people may find upsetting.

## Macbeth
### by William Shakespeare and A.N. Other

IMPORTANT NOTE: All the words in italics in this script were written by Shakespeare (honest!). All the words written in normal type are by A.N. Other.

### Scene 4 Macduff's castle

| | |
|---|---|
| Narrator: | Macbeth was a nasty man who killed the king and took his throne. Then he set out to kill his other enemies … especially the noble Macduff. First he sent a couple of murderers to Macduff's castle … |
| Murderer: | *Where is your husband?* |
| Lady Macduff: | *In no such place as thou may find him.* |
| Murderer: | *He is a traitor.* |
| Young Macduff: | *Thou liest, thou shag-haired villain!* |
| Murderer: | *What, you egg!* |
| | (And the murderer stabs young Macduff) |

YOU'RE FOR IT NOW SONNY! I HAPPEN TO BE VERY SENSITIVE ABOUT MY SHAG HAIR!

**Young Macduff:** *He has killed me, mother.* (Yes. This line really is in the printed play. But it's hard to believe witty Will really wrote it.) *Run away, I pray you!*

(Lady Macduff runs away, chased by the murderer. Screams off stage tell us that he caught her.)

**Lady Macduff:** Help! They've caught me! Ouch!

**Narrator:** When Macduff heard about his family's death, he came back home to Scotland for revenge! Macbeth was left to face Macduff alone …

(Macduff enters waving a sword)

**Macduff:** *Tyrant, show thy face!*

**Macbeth:** *Of all men else I have avoided thee, My soul is too much charged with blood of thine.*

**Macduff:** *I have no words; My voice is in my sword.*

(They fight and Macduff kills Macbeth)

**Narrator:** And so Macduff killed Macbeth.

| | |
|---|---|
| Macbeth: | I guess that serves me right. |
| Macduff: | So, that's the end of rotten old Macbeth. |
| | And now it's to the pub to celebrate! |
| Narrator: | The end! |

*Did you know…?*
Shakespeare used nearly 18,000 different words while the Bible of that time only used about 8,000.

# Snooty snobs

As long as there have been words there have been snobs. Snobs are people who use words to show they are better than you. They can do this by using *bigger* words or they can do it by *pronouncing* their words differently. Now, with the power of words, you can fight back!

**Sesquipedalian verbiage (words that are half a metre long!)**
We've seen how English words have come from all over the world. So, it's not unusual to find there are several words to describe the same thing …

For example, *big* can be *huge* (from the old French), *gigantic* (from the Latin), *titanic* (from the Greek) not to mention *tremendous*, *vast*, *immense* and so on. Take your pick!

So English speakers can have some fun switching words in well-known rhymes or songs.

A popular song of the 1940s was called, *Show me the way to go home*. It was often sung by comedians who were acting drunk.

However, by the 1960s some wordily wicked people had changed the words. Here are the two versions side by side – the original one and the one that may be sung by an English teacher (who is acting drunk).

| Original | Drunken English teacher |
|---|---|
| Show me the way to go home. | Indicate the approach to my habitual abode |
| I'm tired and I want to go to bed. | I'm fatigued and I wish to seek repose. |
| I had a little drink about an hour ago | I'd intoxicating liquor sixty minutes ago |
| And it's gone right to my head. | And it's gone straight to my cranium. |
| No matter where I roam, | No matter where I may perambulate, |
| On land, on sea or foam, | On land, on sea or on effervescent liquid, |
| You can always hear me singing this song. | You can always hear me reciting this refrain |
| Show me the way to go home. | Indicate the approach to my habitual abode |

## Talking proper

It's not just what you say that matters. It can also be the way you say it. Your accent. Even in the Middle Ages people who came from London thought they spoke English 'better' than anyone else. If you spoke it with another accent then you were either low class or low-brained. So people started to speak with a south of England accent to try to impress people. Five hundred years later they are still doing it.

In 1954 someone spotted that 'lower-class' and 'upper-class' people could be separated by the *choice of words*. If you were 'upper-class' then you were said to be 'U'. Lower class people, of course, were 'Non-U'. The language expert, A.S.C. Ross, listed words that were 'U' and 'Non-U'.

If you'd wanted to be posh in the 1950s you'd have to know the difference. Here is a guide ...

**Upper-class people say: While lower-class people say:**

SICK
LAVATORY
RIDING
PUDDING
LOOKING-GLASS
SCOTCH
WRITING-PAPER
LUNCHEON

ILL
TOILET
HORSE RIDING
SWEET
MIRROR
SCOTTISH
NOTE-PAPER
DINNER

*Did you know…?*
The people of London might have thought they were better than the people from the rest of the country. But the people from the country had a poor view of Londoners. They compared them to a cockerel's egg – something unnatural and weird. The Middle English word for eggs was 'eyen', so Londoners were called 'cock-eyen'. Today they are still proud to be called 'Cockney' – maybe they don't realize it's actually an insult!

# Suffering spelling

## Having a bad spell

Once upon a time there was a class of fifteen-year-old boys. They were not very good at English. In fact they were not much good at anything – but they were worse at English.

One day an inspector walked into the classroom. The teacher was terrified. (Inspectors have this effect on teachers). 'What are they doing?' the inspector asked.

'Um ... er ... oh ... er ... English!' the poor teacher babbled.

'Ahhh!' the inspector sighed. 'The beauties of our language. I used to be an English teacher myself, before I escaped from the classroom,' he grinned.

The teacher swallowed hard. There's nothing worse than an ex-teacher telling you where you are going wrong. 'They're not very good,' the teacher explained.

'Let me look. I'll see if I can offer any advice,' the inspector offered and began to walk around the classroom looking over the shoulders of the pupils.

He stopped at Gary's desk. He leaned forward. 'What's your name, son?' he asked.

'*Sniff!* ...Gary,' the boy said. (He was pleased because that was the first question he'd got right this week.)

'May I read this to the rest of the class?' the inspector smiled.

'*Sniff!* …You what?' Gary said and used his sleeve instead of a handkerchief.

'This poem. I want to read it to the class, if that's all right with you.'

'*Sniff!* … But …' Gary began to explain. The inspector wasn't listening. He picked up the book and turned to the class.

'Listen everyone. Put your pens down, stop writing and listen.'

The boys turned and looked at this strange man. Mouths hung open and the only sound was of noses dribbling.

'Gary here has written a poem. A quite beautiful poem, I think, about the meaning of life. It is a lesson to all of us. I want to read it to you, if I may.'

The man walked to the front of the class. He held up the exercise book and read in a commanding voice.

137

The man's voice had sunk to a whisper by the end. He passed the book gently back to Gary. 'A wonderful, meaningful poem, Gary.'

'*Sniff*!' Gary sniffed. 'It's not a poem, sir … them's me spelling corrections!'

*Did you know…?*

There have been many attempts to make English spelling simple. The most successful one was by the American, Noah Webster, who wrote the first American Dictionary. He changed *colour* to *color*, *centre* to *center* and *traveller* to *traveler*, for example – that's how the Americans now spell those words. He dropped the 'k' off the end of words like *musick* and *magick* – and that's how everyone now spells them. He also dropped the 'e' off the end of medicine and examine … but that idea never caught on. He wanted the law to punish people who refused to spell the American way!

Of course, there is nothing new in this idea. English teachers have been punishing pupils for hundreds of years for not spelling their way!

## Simpler spelling 1

The Simplified Spelling Society almost succeeded in changing the way we spell in Britain. In 1949 their ideas were put to Parliament but were thrown out – only by 87 votes to 84. But what was the title of their book?

1 *New Spelling.*
2 *Nue Spelling.*
3 *New Spelin.*

*Answer:* 2 *Nue Spelling.* A 1953 Act of Parliament to change spelling passed its first stage before it was finally defeated. Just as well ... uther-whys wee cud orl bee spelin peck-yoo-leah.

## Simpler Spelling 2

In 1906 a rich American called Andrew Carnegie gave $250,000 to set up the Simplified Spelling Board. They sorted out words like *program* and *catalog* but had *troble* with others. No one wanted their *yu* for 'you' and the board died. As its members would have written ... *tuf.*

**Heard this one?**
*Beware of heard, a dreadful word,*
*That looks like beard and sounds like bird,*
*And dead; it's said like bed, not bead,*
*For goodness sake, don't call it deed!*
*Watch out for meat and great and threat,*
*They rhyme with suite and straight and debt.*

*Did you know…?*
Rearrange the letters in William Shakespeare and you get
'I am a weakish speller!' … which is true!

## A spell in prison

So you think your spelling is poor? What about the London
police? Here are a few of the mistakes that have appeared in
their reports over the past ten years …

- 'Mr Brown reported that his garden gnombs had been
  stolen.'
- 'The suspect was wearing a car key jacket.'
- 'He climbed on the roof and forced open the skylark.'
- 'The victim was wearing a pale blue suite.'
- 'I stopped a man wearing a leather berry on his head.'

## A spell in school

But before your teachers start laughing at the poor plods, read this letter to *The Times* newspaper ...

Dear Sir

When my son started at his comprehensive school in 1972 I was told by his English teacher that spelling was not taught because it did not matter.

A teacher at my daughter's Primary School took a different view. He thought spelling did matter. When he came across the word "medycine" in my daughter's work he sternly changed it to "medecine".

And at one time teachers taught wrong spelling deliberately! There was a reading scheme in the 1960s where words were spelled as they looked – fox would be spelled *focks* or *foks*. Eventually the poor pupils transferred to normal spellings. It didn't work too well. In fact many people said that, for the children, it was *katustrofik*.

# Slobbish slang

Slang words or phrases are used instead of the real ones to make an idea more interesting ... or shocking!

Very often people in authority don't understand slang ... and don't approve! That only makes the slang-talkers do it more! Especially if it is the slang of young people and it's parents or teachers who don't approve. (**Note:** when teachers and parents use their own special words they call it *jargon* because that is much more agreeable.)

How does it feel to be an outsider trying to understand someone else's slang? Find out. What would you say, yes or no, if someone said to you ...

1 'Do you own a *weasel?*'

2 'Will you pop your head into that lion's *dining room?*'
3 'Would you like to introduce my *bunch of sprouts* to your *cauliflower?*'

142

4 'Have you ever had a slice of *grunting peck*?'
5 'If you looked in a mirror would you see a *jobbernowl*?'
6 'Have you ever seen a *podgy* teacher?'
7 'Would you like a room full of *sausage and mash*?'

8 'Fancy a picnic in the *marble orchard*?'
9 'Would you like a two-week holiday at *The Queen's Inn*?'
10 'Lend me your baseball cap, I need a *technicolour yawn*!'

*Answers:* 1 *weasel* = coat (20th-century London rhyming slang – *weasel and stoat*) 2 *dining room* = mouth. (England 19th century) 3 *bunch of sprouts* = fist (19th century); *cauliflower* = ear (20th century) 4 *grunting peck* = pork (England 16th century) 5 *jobbernowl* = fool's head (England 16th century) 6 *podgy* = drunken (England 18th century) 7 *sausage and mash* = cash (19th-century London rhyming slang) 8 *marble orchard* = graveyard (USA, late 19th century) 9 *The Queen's Inn* = prison (18th century) 10 *technicolour yawn* = vomit. (Australia 1960s)

143

*Did you know…?*

The slang word *gob* for mouth is over 500 years old. It came from an Irish word meaning 'beak'. So next time someone annoys you then it is more polite to say 'Shut your beak!' than 'Shut your gob!' … though it still means the same thing.

## Old slang

In the 1700s there were villainous children who enjoyed breaking windows by throwing half-pence coins at them. These window-breakers were knows as *nickers*.

# Shocking swear words

## Five flipping fascinating facts

**1** In 1623 the English Parliament passed a law making it illegal to swear. You were fined for saying shocking things like, *by my troth*, or the unspeakably rude, *upon my life*.

**2** It couldn't last, of course. In 1649 the laws were changed. After that swearing was punishable by *death!*

**3** Samuel Johnson wrote a dictionary in 1755 and missed out any naughty words. A lady said to him one day, 'I am pleased to see you have missed the rude words from your dictionary.' Doctor Johnson grinned and said wickedly, 'Ah, so you've been looking for them, have you?'

**4** In 1818 Thomas Bowdler rewrote Shakespeare's plays … without all the swear words and naughty bits. (People who mess with books in this way are now said to *Bowdler*ize them.)

**5** People sometimes use words without realizing how disgusting they are. We sometimes call useless bits of paper, *bumf* – in fact it's a shortened form of the word, *bumfodder*. And that isn't useless paper at all … it is toilet paper, in fact! And many polite people quite happily call a piece of nonsense, *poppycock*. Would they still use the word if they knew it was from the Dutch word for 'soft cow droppings'?

## Careful curses

The trouble with swearing is that it can get you into trouble. There is only one way round this. Come up with some *really old* curses. *You* know what they mean … but no one else does. That way you can express your feelings without upsetting people!

Here are some genuine nasty words for your use in an emergency. Can you guess what they mean before you check out the answers?

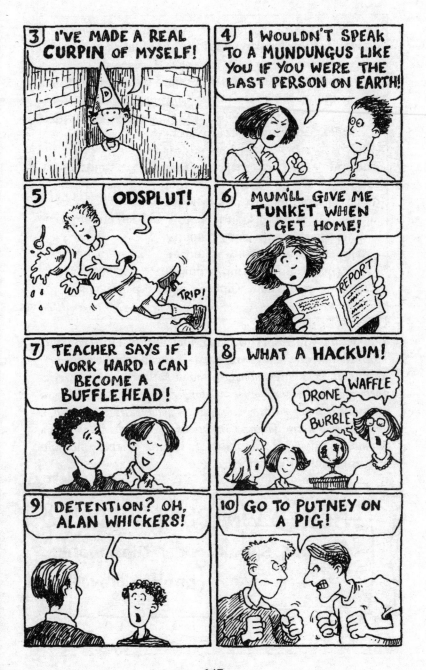

*Answers:*

1 Golter-yeded: Old English curse of unknown meaning (but it sounds great!)
2 Fumet: Technical word for deer droppings
3 Curpin: Middle English for chicken's bum.
4 Mundungus: Middle English word for smelly rubbish (and later to describe cheap tobacco smoke)
5 Odsplut: Early modern English – probably from 'God's Blood' curse.
6 Tunket: Early American word for 'Hell'
7 Buttlehead: 17th-century for idiot
8 Hackum: 17th-century for a big-mouth
9 Alan Whickers: 20th-century rhyming slang for knickers
10 Go to Putney on a pig: 19th-century expression for 'Go to hell.'

But before you resort to using such disgraceful language, stop! If someone upsets you then *don't* call them a *honyoker*, a *mudsill*, a *ninnyhammer*, a *quakebuttock*, a *ballarag*, a *borborygmite*, a *gongoozler*, a *dunderwhelp*, a *cockabaloo*, a *lobscouse*, a *humgruffin*, a *gundygut*, a *noddypole*, a *ragabash*, a *smellfungus*, a *trollybags*, a *twittletwattle*, a *yazzihamper*, a *scomm*, a *scroyle* or a *skellum* … or any of the other old English insults. Remember …

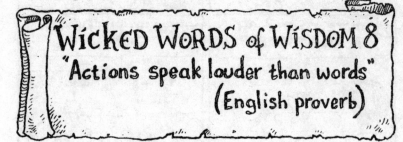

WICKED WORDS of WISDOM 8
"Actions speak louder than words"
(English proverb)

… and get *revenge!*

# Silly Spooner

The Reverend William Spooner was a clergyman at New College Oxford from 1903 till 1924. A very boring and totally forgettable man ... except that he had a habit of *metaphasis*. (Yes, that's another of those boring words about words. But after Doc Spooner got his mouth around words then *metaphasis* became known as Spoonerisms!)

He mixed up the sounds at the beginning of words. So what? So he came up with some comical mistakes. Instead of saying, 'Show me to another seat because someone is occupying my pew,' he was likely to say, 'Sew me to another sheet because someone is occupewing my pie!'

What did he mean when he said to a bad student ...

and

Even his *thinking* was a little bit scrambled. He once approached a student and said:

The truth is that people were writing Spoonerisms before the Reverend Spooner was even born. Shakespeare's Grumio in *Taming of the Shrew* says, 'The oats have eaten the horses.' A 1622 book describes how a man in an inn wanted to say, 'I must go and buy a dagger,' but said, 'I must go and dye a beggar.' A character in an 1854 novel (published when Spooner was just a boy) took out a tobacco pouch and invited his friend to 'poke a smipe'.

Poor Spooner never enjoyed being laughed at. He thighed in nineteen-dirty.

THINGS JUST HAVEN'T BEEN THE SAME HERE SINCE WE PUT OLD SPOONER IN CHARGE OF THE STAFF CANTEEN...

Today's Menu

Chish & Fips
Mangers & Bash
Pieherd's Shep
Hot, tuttered boast

A Cug of Moffee
or
A nice Tot of Pea

## Spooner-type joke – 1

Once upon a time a little girl came into the kitchen and found her mother crying. 'What's the matter, mummy?' she asked.

'I've just had some bad news,' the moaning mother said. 'Old Mr Spilk next door has died.'

'Old Mr Spilk?' the girl gasped. 'That lovely old man that I called Uncle Milt?'

'That's him.'

'It's sad,' the little girl agreed. 'But you shouldn't cry, mummy!'

'Why not?' the wailing woman wept.

'Because you always tell me ... it's no use crying over Milt Spilk!'

## Spooner-type joke – 2

An aeroplane was flying over London when a door flew open and a crate fell out. The crate was full of those little wheels with teeth that fit into gearboxes.

The little wheels fell from the sky and bounced off the heads of the unlucky people below. The police were called to investigate and Detective Sergeant Shirley Holmes raced to the scene. She picked up a little wheel and looked at it through her magnifying glass. 'As I thought. These come from a Japanese car!' she said.

'How do you know?' PC Watson gasped.

'Elementary, my dear Watson,' Holmes said. 'It's just been raining Datsun cogs!'

151

## Spooner-mania

Spoonerisms can be catching. This charming little
story becomes a road of lot if you get too fond of
Spoonerisms …

> One day I took out my well-boiled icicle and went
> for a ride. Then it started roaring with pain. My
> tireless tube burst and a cat popped on its drawers
> in front of me! I swerved but struck the cat a
> blushing crow! The cat ran off with a witty-full
> pail.

Me what I seen?

# Terrible tongue-twisters

Some words were never meant to go with other words. They are too difficult to say together. So, just to torture other people, wicked wordsters have put those words together into tongue-twisters. They were very popular with Victorian children, but some are still recited today.

Have a competition with some friends. Time yourselves reading these wicked Victorian tongue-twisters aloud. Anyone who can do one in under ten seconds is good – all five in under 50 seconds is a genius! But be careful … if you make a mistake you must go back to the start of the tongue-twister …

1

2

**3**

IRON COFFEE POTS AND TIN COFFEE POTS
THEY'RE NO USE TO ME
IF I CAN'T HAVE A PROPER CUP OF COFFEE
   FROM A PROPER COPPER COFFEE POT
I'LL HAVE A CUP OF TEA

**4**

A FLY AND A FLEA IN A FLUE
WERE IMPRISONED, SO WHAT COULD THEY DO?
SAID THE FLY "LET US FLEA!" SAID THE FLEA
                    "LET US FLY!"
SO THEY FLEW THROUGH A FLAW IN THE FLUE

PHEW!

**5**

SISTER SUSIE'S SEWING SHIRTS FOR SOLDIERS
SUCH SKILL AT SEWING SHIRTS OUR SHY YOUNG
                    SISTER SUSIE SHOWS
SOME SOLDIERS SEND EPISTLES, SAY THEY'D
                    SOONER SLEEP IN THISTLES
THAN THE SAUCY, SOFT, SHORT SHIRTS FOR
                    SOLDIERS SISTER SUSIE SEWS

WICKED WORDS of WISDOM 9
"Don't tie a knot in your tongue that you cannot undo with your teeth."
(Portuguese proverb)

(Remember it … just don't ask me what it means.)

# United States of America

## History of the language – part 6

Just when some English teachers thought the word invasions were over, along came a new one. The United States of America came along and started adding to the English language!

As the English-speaking people moved across America they discovered new plants and animals so they had to have new names for them; they created new jobs, new inventions and new things to do … including new crimes. All of these things needed new *words*.

Some of these American-English words are so familiar we often forget they are fairly new. But, do you know *how* new? Here are some words from America you'll be familiar with. Can you guess when they were first used?

*Answers*:

Mugging – **1** The word was used by the gruesome gangs that wandered the New York streets. They had fearsome names like The Plug Uglies and the Dead Rabbits. How would you like to be mugged by a Dead Rabbit?

Joy-ride – **3** In Britain today a joy-ride is usually in a stolen car. In USA in 1909 it meant exactly – a *joyful* ride in an automobile – an 1899 name for the petrol-driven carriage. Other 'car' names included *horseless carriage*, *autopher*, *autovic*, *autobat*, *diamote*, *self-motor* and simply *machine*. The car manufacturers also had some exciting names – *Cadillac* survived. Some that didn't last include *Bugmobile*, *Black Crow*, *Averageman's car*, the *Lone Star*, the *Hupmobile* and the *Locomobile*. Would you like to boast to your friends, 'Dad's got a Black Crow in the garage!'

GEE – I WONDER WHY THEY CALL THIS A BUGMOBILE...

BUZZZZZZZz

Coca-Cola – **2** In 1886 a chemist called John Styth Pemberton brewed up leaves from the coca plant, nuts from the cola plant and a few other things in an old iron tub in his back garden. He stirred it with a wooden paddle from a boat and created a drink which would cure headaches and other illnesses. He called it Coca-Cola and sold the recipe for under $300. When it was sold 30 years later it was valued at $25 *million!* It is still growing in spite of a couple of disastrous experiments. One was *New Coke* introduced in 1985 ... and the other was Coca-Cola flavoured cigars!

Movies – 3 People were calling films *moving pictures* in 1896 but by 1900 everyone had shortened it to *movies* in the USA – *pictures* in the UK. This was better than the name some early film-makers gave their shows. One called his *mechanically reproduced theatre entertainment*. In 1912 the Essanay film studios were worried that the word *movies* was a little bit low class and had a competition to choose a new name. What would *you* have invented? The winner was *photoplay*, but it never caught on.

Craze – 2 *Craze* used to mean cracked or broken but by 1820 it had come to mean something incredibly popular. Over the years there have been thousands of *crazes* in America. In the 1860s it was roller skating (from Holland) and about a hundred years later (late 1970s) it was skateboarding. Imagine that! It took 100 years to discover you could throw one roller skate away and play on the other!

THIS NEW CRAZE IS DEAD BORING!

I THINK YOU'RE ONLY MEANT TO THROW AWAY ONE ROLLER-SKATE...

Airmail – **2** The Wright Brothers had made the first aeroplane flight in 1903 and within 15 years some mail was being delivered by air. The trouble was that it wasn't very safe. The government hired 40 pilots to fly the airmail planes – but most of the flights were at night and 31 of the pilots died in crashes. The letters probably had a rough ride too. Within a few years there were another couple of charming new words – *airsick* and *airbag*. (Remember this when your friends boast that their new car has an *airbag* – the first *airbags* were for catching the *airsick!*)

Telephone – **1** Trick question! The instrument we call the telephone was invented in 1876 by Alexander Graham Bell ... but he didn't invent the word. It had been in use for 40 years to describe machines that gave a message over a long distance – a really loud foghorn had been called a telephone for example. Bell spoke those famous first telephoned words to his assistant, 'Mr Watson, come here, I want you.' You can re-enact that famous piece of history at any time ... so long as you know someone called Mr Watson, of course.

Skyscraper – **1** Oh, no! *Another* trick question! The first *building* to be named a *skyscraper* was the Home Insurance Building in Chicago in 1888. But the word had been around since at least 1794 to describe a top hat or the tallest mast of a ship. Imagine walking around with a *skyscraper* on your head!

Santa Claus – **2** The Americans didn't invent Santa Claus, of course. But they were the first to start to use the Dutch name, *Sinter Klaas*, meaning Saint Nicholas, to describe Father Christmas. Were they grateful to the Dutch settlers for Santa Claus? They were not! They took the Dutch settlement of New Amsterdam (named after the Dutch capital) and changed it to New York (named after the Duke of York). Let that be a lesson to you about lending the Americans words. You will get no thanks.

Tobacco – **1** Another of those borrowed words. The Spanish named it *tobacco* first. In 1565 John Hawkins took some back to England and told everybody what a wonderful herb it was. By the time people discovered that it actually kills you it was too late. People were making a fortune out of the stuff!

These are just ten of the thousands of words that the English language in the world has adopted from the English language of America. It's not surprising that British speakers of English are worried that the Americans are taking over. There are about 240 million Americans using the language – other English speakers all added together don't make 100 million.

American words are here to stay! … as sure as Coca-Cola, skyscrapers, Santa Claus and telephones are here to stay.

The United States now has a weapon greater than the Roman Legions, mightier than the Anglo-Saxon sword, more powerful than the Norman Knights … something called television! In its early days television was also known as *radio vision, electric eye, iconoscope* and *electric telescope.* Does it matter? As Shakespeare said, *What's in a name? … a rose by any other name would smell as sweet.* Or, as he might have said, *An electric telescope by any other name would still show repeats.*

# Vile verse

*Among our many English rhymes*
*There's none, they say, for month.*
*I've tried and failed a hundred times –*
*Then made it the hundred and onth!*

## Pathetic poetry

A very clever poet called Samuel Taylor Coleridge wrote, 'Poetry; the *best* words in the best order.' It is true that *some* poetry can move you to tears. What Coleridge should have said was '*Good* poetry; the best words in the best order.'

Because the world's worst poetry can also be the world's worst use of words. It can be seriously wicked. It can move you to tears … of *laughter.*

Not comic poems, you understand. Not the poems that are deliberately funny. Comic poems can be perfect examples of the 'best words in the best order.' This one is one of the shortest poems written and it doesn't waste a single word …

*Little dog,*
*Crossing street,*
*Motor car,*
*Sausage meat.*

The poems that are supposed to be serious can be the funniest. Here is a selection of pathetic poetry. Read them and weep …

163

## Six of the worst

**1** Bad poets seem to think their poems have to *rhyme*. This just adds to the drama of this tragic tale of disappointed love by Lilian Curtis (19th-century USA)

*I loved the gentle girl*
*But oh, I heaved a sigh,*
*When first she told me she could see*
*Out of only one eye.*

**2** Since Charles II, the monarchs of Britain have appointed someone to be the 'Royal Poet' ... then their title became 'Poet Laureate'. The job involves writing special verses for royal occasions. Unfortunately winning this title seems to have a disastrous effect on the poets. Good poets become pretty awful ... and awful poets go from bad to verse!

The most despised Poet Laureate was probably Laurence Eusden (1688–1730). In his poem, *Hero and Leander*, the hero (who is called Leander) loves the heroine (who is called Hero). Got that? Every night he swims across the sea to see her. One night he drowns. After nearly 500 lines of Eusden's drivel we expect a tearful climax. What we get is Hero searching for Leander ...

> *But ah! Too soon she spied him, where he lay,*
> *A lump of beautiful, though breathless clay.*

3 Not all poets used gentle words to describe a tragic death. When James Henry Powell's friend lost a drunken brother on a railway track he wrote …

> *Thy mangled corpse upon the rails*
> *in frightful shape was found,*
> *The ponderous train had killed thee*
> *as its wheels went round.*

4 James Grainger (1721–1766) combined the blood and guts of the Powell poem with the drama of the Leander story. A young man saw his sweetheart waiting for him on the shore of a West Indian island. He couldn't wait for the ship to reach the harbour. He flung himself over the side and swam towards her. How romantic! Until …

*Then through the white surf she did haste*
*When, ah! A shark bit through his waist.*
*He shrieked! He half-sprung from the wave,*
*Streaming with purple gore,*
*And soon found it a living grave*
*And ah! Was seen no more.*

**5** Most students of English agree that Scottish poet William McGonagall was probably the worst poet ever to publish in the English language. It wasn't just the way he mangled words. It was the awful subjects he wrote about. The title is truly sad ... *Calamity in London – family of ten burned to death* ... but the poem is truly, hilariously bad ...

*Oh, heaven! It was a frightful and pitiful sight to see*
*Seven bodies charred of the Jarvis family;*
*And Mrs Jarvis found with her child,*
*    and both carbonised,*
*And as the searchers gazed thereon they*
*    were surprised.*
*And these were lying beside the fragments of the bed,*
*And in a chair the tenth victim was sitting dead;*
*Oh horrible! Oh, horrible! What a sight to behold,*
*The charred and burnt bodies of young and old.*

Frightful, pitiful and horrible ... and that's just McGonagall's poetry!

**6** It helps if a poem has a title, you may have noticed. Especially a *bad* poem. This poem by Amanda McKitterick Ros is puzzling if you don't know the title. What is it describing? A battlefield? A slaughterhouse? What do you think?

> *Holy Moses! Take a look!*
> *Flesh decayed in every nook,*
> *Some rare bits of brain lie here,*
> *Mortal loads of beef and beer.*

Did you guess? The title is *On Visiting Westminster Abbey*. (However, don't let this poem put you off visiting the abbey – the 'rare bits of brain' and 'flesh decayed' are well hidden under stone tombs.)

*Did you know…?*
The longest poem published was John Fitchett's *King Alfred*. It lasted 129,807 boring lines, took 40 years to write … and Fitchett died in 1838 before he could finish it. King Alfred's cake-burning episode was described …

> *The ancient dame bids him with care attend*
> *Some oaten cakes then baking on the hearth.*
> *Alas! The cakes forgot soon show a heap*
> *All black, memorials of his sad neglect.*

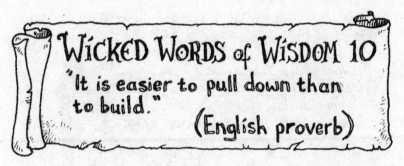

WICKED WORDS of WISDOM 10
"It is easier to pull down than
to build."
(English proverb)

So, instead of laughing at those pathetic poets, why not write some pathetic poetry yourself and give the world even more laughs?

# Wicked words to test your teacher

Test your teacher! Each of these rare words has been given two definitions. Can he/she/it work out which is the true one?

**1** *Adamitism*
**a)** believing that all children are good and kind
**b)** running around with no clothes on because it's against your religion

**2** *Business*
**a)** a collection of ferrets
**b)** a very nosey person

**3** *Drack*
**a)** an Australian slang word for someone who looks like the vampire Dracula
**b)** a Transylvanian silver coin (with the image of Count Dracula on it)

**4** *Coprolite*
**a)** a type of monk
**b)** fossilized animal droppings

**5** *Eructation*
**a)** extreme intelligence (like a teacher who decides to retire)
**b)** burping till the windows in a room tremble

**6** *Fustanella*
**a)** a skirt worn by a Greek man
**b)** a character in a novel by Charles Dickens

**7** *Glabrous*
**a)** as bald as an alligator's egg
**b)** feverish and hot

**8** *Hoppo–bumpo*
**a)** an Indian name for a three-legged elephant
**b)** a hopping game where players try to barge their opponents to the ground

**9** *Ig-man*
**a)** somebody rather stupid (and ignorant)
**b)** an Eskimo (who lives in an igloo)

**10** *Jonnop*
**a)** Australian slang for a policeman
**b)** a small pony used by small riders for hunting fox cubs

**11** *Kippage*
**a)** a state of great excitement
**b)** a sleeping cabin on a steam ship

**12** *Logorrhoea*
**a)** talking too much and not being able to stop
**b)** a liver disease that comes from drinking too much coke

**13** *Muckender*
**a)** an old word for a handkerchief
**b)** a Medieval rubbish collector

**14** *Nogging*
**a)** a 16th-century punishment for schoolboys
**b)** material used to stuff up the cracks in a log cabin

**15** *Obumbrated*
**a)** sitting on something very sticky and becoming fixed
**b)** covered by a shadow (sort of umbrellarated)

**16** *Putto*
**a)** a small boy, but usually a baby angel in a painting
**b)** Victorian modelling clay for rich children

**17** *Qar*
**a)** an Australian police car (a Q–car, geddit?)
**b)** a spider found in South America and crushed to make
purple food–dye

EEEk!

POLICE

**18** *Rushbuckler*
**a)** the Austrian name for a German Shepherd dog
**b)** a Tudor name for a rough, tough and violent young man

**19** *Slutch*
**a)** a slovenly female
**b)** a drain used to keep canals clean

**20** *Tittery*
**a)** a place where small, green-and-yellow birds nest together
**b)** strong drink that will make you tottery

**21** *Umslopogus*
**a)** someone who spills school dinner down their shirt
**b)** the name of a Zulu chief in a novel by Rider Haggard

**22** *Vom*
**a)** bad food (that makes you want to vomit)
**b)** a 1950s motor car made in Czechoslovakia

173

**23** *Woodpusher*
**a)** a teacher with a particularly thick class
**b)** a particularly thick chess player

**24** *Xanthic*
**a)** having a yellowish colour (like a traffic warden's cap)
**b)** colour-blind (and unable to tell a traffic warden from a bus conductor)

**25** *Yehudi*
**a)** American slang for someone who is always fiddling about (after violin player Yehudi Menuhin)
**b)** a Medieval Persian prince who invented dog-shows

**26** *Zumbooruk*
**a)** a Turkish three-masted sailing ship
**b)** a small cannon fired from the back of a camel

Check your teacher's score:

26 = cheat!
20+ = brilliant
13 = average
8– = should be sent to bed with a dictionary
3– = anyone that unlucky shouldn't be allowed out of the house

# X-words

The world's first crossword appeared in the *New York World* newspaper in 1913. But do you know what its inventor called it?

1 Word search
2 Crossword puzzle
3 Word Cross puzzle

*Answer:* 3 The inventor was an Englishman called Arthur Wynne. Wynne by name ... but loser when it came to picking a name for his puzzle!

**Wynne's wonderful word cross**

## CLUES

### Across

2–3 What bargain hunters enjoy

4–5 A written acknowledgement

6–7 Such and nothing more

### Down

10–18 The fibre of the gomuti palm

6–22 What we all should be

4–26 A day dream

**Across**

10-11 A bird
14-15 Opposed to less
18-19 What this puzzle is
22-23 An animal of prey
26-27 The close of a day
28-29 To elude
30-31 The plural of is
8-9 To cultivate
12-13 A bar of wood or iron
16-17 What artists learn to do
20-21 Fastened
24-25 Found on the seashore

**Down**

2-11 A talon
19-28 A pigeon
F-7 Part of your head
23-30 A river in Russia
1-32 To govern
33-34 An aromatic plant
N-8 A fist
24-31 To agree with
3-12 Part of a ship
20-29 One
5-27 Exchanging
9-25 To sink in mud
13-21 A boy

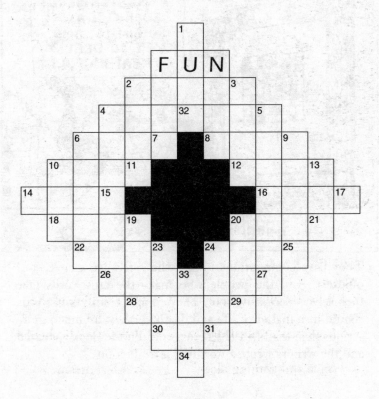

177

## Cross people

Many people take crosswords very seriously.

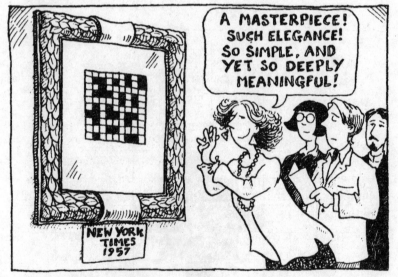

They have competitions to see who can solve a crossword
quickest. And the people who make the crosswords take
themselves seriously too. They don't think crosswords
should be a matter of life and death ... they are much more
serious than that! In 1924 a crossword Puzzle Book appeared
and the writers wrote a warming introduction ...

# THIS IS NOT A TOY!

## To fathers and mothers, uncles and aunts

It is just possible you may pick up this book thinking of it as a present for the younger children. Will you please do us one favour – in the name of humanity? Just solve half a dozen of the puzzles yourself, before you pass it on. It's a small thing to ask – you'll be able to go back to your work in about a week.

So there!

*Did you know…?*

The largest crossword ever created was written by Hristo A. Yonitsov. The record was set in Bulgaria on 3 June 2014. The crossword is 300 metres long, spread over 1000 sheets of paper and has 93,769 clues. It took Hristo 14 years to complete, with many of the words being found during trips to the library.

# Y-drunken

*Y-drunken* is just one way of saying *drunk*. The amazing truth is there are so many other ways of saying *drunk* you could fill a book with them.

And in 1733, that's just what the American statesman and author, Benjamin Franklin, did. He brought out the *Drinker's Dictionary* with 228 words that mean *drunk*. But in 1983 the author of a book called *Words* claimed a world record when he collected 2,231 of them. Here is an alphabet of words and phrases – only an 'X' word is missing. They all mean drunk …

# Zee end ... or is it?

That brings us to zee end of zis book. In the immortal words of Mrs Julia A. Moore ...

*And now, kind friends, what I have wrote*
*I hope you will pass o'er,*
*And not criticise, as some have done,*
*Hitherto herebefore.*

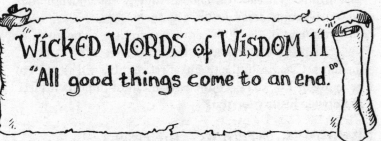

WICKED WORDS of WISDOM 11
"All good things come to an end."

... even a Horrible History book but ...

"All's well that ends well."

... especially if you've enjoyed the book. If you haven't enjoyed it then don't cry about it because ...

"Laugh and the world laughs with you, cry and you cry alone..."

But, of course, that's not the end of the history of the English Language. That goes on changing and flowing all the time – a bit like a river. You have to keep up with it if you want to stay in control of your life.

Remember what I said in the introduction. Words have power. Power to change people's minds and their thinking. You can use their power to hurt – or you can be hurt by them.

In the past the power of words always lay in the hands of the upper classes who could read and write. Now it lies in *your* hands. But can you choose your words and use your power so people don't get hurt by them?

At the end of the 20th century there is a name given to this thoughtful use of words. 'Political Correctness' – or PC for short. Citizens of the twenty-first century will all need to be aware of PC, so here's the last and most important piece of horrible history for you.

## Political Correctness – the rules

Everyone is equal. (If you don't agree then it might be better if you skip this section!) Just because you are taller than your brother does not mean you are better. So, don't call him 'titch', 'shorty', or 'midget'. He is simply being 'challenged' to grow a little more in the 'vertical' direction … call him vertically challenged.

And men and women are equal. So, don't use the word 'man' when the word could just as easily apply to a woman. Use 'person' – or drop 'man' altogether. A 'chairman' of a meeting can be a 'chairperson' or simply a 'chair'.

Of course this takes a bit of getting used to. Some of the PC words don't always trip off the tongue at first ...

CAN I HAVE A PLOUGH-PERSON'S LUNCH, PLEASE?

Get the idea? No? Then perhaps you are stupid ... oops! Sorry! 'Mentally challenged'?

**Learn some PC terms ...**
**1 Emotionally different** – a pleasant way to describe a 'mad' or 'crazy' person, as in, 'I was punched on the nose by an emotionally different person!'
**2 Environmental hygienist** – someone who keeps your environment hygienically clean; someone like the person who runs your school! (No, I mean the caretaker, not the head-teacher!)
**3 Hair disadvantaged** – some people are embarrassed by being without hair on their heads. (It never bothered Medieval monks but it bothers some modern men.) So, when you watch Star Trek with a hair-disadvantaged person ... do NOT say their mission is 'to baldly go ...' And never call them 'slaphead'.

WHAT A HAIR-RAISING EPISODE!... OOOOOOOOPS...

CAPTAIN, IT'S.... AAARGH!

**4 Prewoman** – those people you share a classroom with are *not* 'girls'. Females aged 11 or under are *prewomen*. And, if you are a pre*man*, never ever call your prewoman friend 'baby', 'chick', 'darling', or 'love'.

**5 Hystery or Herstory** – you are *not* reading a 'Horrible History' (never mind what it says on the un-PC cover of this book.) His story is also Her story so let's use these new words. (Note: But don't worry too much about this one – and don't go scribbling the word from the cover of your school book. Our word 'history' comes from the Greek word 'investigate' – it has nothing to do with his, her, its or anybody's story.)

**6 Metabolically different** – someone whose 'metabolism' is different to yours probably suffers from a lack of heart-beat and brain power. They are, frankly, **dead**. However, you would not like to be called 'dead', would you? Be more considerate to corpses. (You may prefer to use the phrase **non-living person.**)

**7 Motivationally deficient** – if you have no motivation then you have no urge to work. Thoughtless teachers call you **lazy**. This is not accurate. If they write *lazy* on your school report you know what to change it to.

**8 Non-traditional shop-per** – the *traditional* shopper will enter a shop, pick up the goods, take them to the assistant and pay for them before leaving the shop. The *non*-traditional shopper will simply omit the paying bit. **Non-traditional shopper** is a much more pleasant term than **shoplifter**, don't you think? (Unless you are the shopkeeper who keeps getting their sweeties nicked!)

**9 Cattle-murderer** – a farmer who keeps cattle to be slaughtered for food. It is probably *not* a good idea to use this PC term to the face of your local farmer. You may throw these cruel words at Farmer Brown but remember ... Farmer Brown probably has something much nastier to throw back. Nastier, smellier, stickier and lying in little piles on the farmyard.

**10 Unwaged labour** – slavery. Anything your mum, dad or teacher orders you to do without pay. 'Wipe the blackboard!', 'Tidy your bedroom!', 'Bury the cat!', 'Go to the chip shop and bring me a small whale with a pineapple ring.' Point an accusing finger and say ...

THAT'S UNWAGED LABOUR... YOU MOTIVATIONALLY DEFICIENT, HAIR-DISADVANTAGED, EMOTIONALLY DIFFERENT PERSON!

**Forget some of these nasty old non-PC words ...**
Becoming a PC word user means giving up some of your old, cruel words. Here are a few suggestions for replacements that you may like to try:

**1 Pet** – Don't insult your cat, dog, hamster or beetle. You wouldn't like to be called 'pet' – it's a bit like being called 'slave'. Call it **animal companion**. (And if you are lucky enough to own a pet rock then consider its feelings too. Call it a **mineral companion**.)

HE'S MY MINERAL COMPANION

**2 Boring** – teachers may be this. But remember – it's not their fault! So be gentle with them. Call them **charm free**.

**3 Ugly** – just because your brother looks like a buffalo's bum there is no need for you to ruin his life by telling him that. Do *not* suggest that he should wear a paper bag over his head. Gently tell him he is **cosmetically different**.

**4 Meat** – let's be honest, this word is a pleasant way to talk about eating dead animals. Why not call it what it is: **flesh**. If you're a vegetarian you eat *non-violent* food. If you want to put your flesh-eating friends off their school dinner of dead hen flesh why not ask, 'How are you enjoying your **scorched corpses of animals?**'

**5 Fat** – there is nothing wrong with being *fat*. Unfortunately the bullies of this world can make life a misery for overweight people. Support your fat friends by agreeing to call them **larger-than-average citizen** or **horizontally challenged** ... or even by ignoring their size altogether!

**6 Books** – and while we're on the subject of cruelty, have you ever thought about the poor tree that died so you could read this page? Let's make all those librarians, teachers and swotty pupils cringe with guilt. Ask them, 'How are you enjoying your **processed tree carcasses?**'

**7 Exams** – we all want to forget that dreadful word. So, go ahead, forget it! In future teachers will assess your *needs*. (Teachers who claim you *need* a good boot up the backside are definitely non-PC!) Look forward to your end of term **needs assessment**.

**8 Smoking** – this is definitely not a PC activity these days. Not only does it kill the smoker but it doesn't do the 'smoked' much good either. So don't report class-mates for 'smoking' – call it what it is: **assault with a deadly weapon.**

**9 Old** – parents and teachers may laugh merrily when you call them 'wrinklies' but deep down they are probably upset. Getting old means getting closer to becoming a non-living human. So, be kind, and call the pensioners in your life **longer-living persons.**

**10 Politically correct** – the *really* bad news is that it is not politically correct to use the term 'politically correct'. Try **culturally sensitive.** Try to remember to forget to say politically correct.

NOW I'M CONFUSED... IS IT YOU-KNOW-WHAT TO SAY YOU-KNOW-WHAT? OR WHAT?

Some of the non–PC words will die away and some of the PC replacements will become normal. Ten years ago your school would have had a headmaster or a headmistress. Now most schools simply have a head-teacher. Ten years ago a woman had to sign herself Miss or Mrs – now she may decide that it makes no difference if she is married or not. After all, men simply call themselves Mr. So now a woman can choose to call herself Ms.

Ten years from now (when you're a longer-living person) you may think nothing of asking for a ploughperson's lunch!

This is the fascinating future. And it's just like the horrible historical past! New words are always being born; they grow, they change and in time they die away. Just like human beings really. That's what makes them so interesting.

If you want to be happy then make friends with human beings. If you want to be *really* happy make friends with wicked words. They can make you shiver with fear or cry out with surprise. They can amaze you, amuse you, alarm and confuse you. They can make you laugh and they can make you weep. But once you get to know them they will hardly ever bore you.

They're wicked!

189

# INTERESTING INDEX

abbreviations (interesting initials) 75, 80-1
accents, 'avin' 133-4
acronyms, manic 80-2
ain't (an American word) 91
algebra (mad maths) 57
alliteration, amazing 17-24
alphabet (rudiments of writing) 31-40, 68, 114, 180
anagrams, argansam 67-71
Anglo-Saxons, awful 13-16, 42, 65, 77, 162
Augustine (Christian Saint) 15

balderdash, boozy 5
Ball, John (English peasant leader) 22-3
beaks, shutting 144
Beowulf (Old English epic) 19-20
Bible 6, 11, 118, 131
Black Death 24
blood 17-23, 55, 78, 128-30
Bowdler, Thomas (English re-writer) 145
bums 47-8, 117, 146, 186
Bush, George (American president) 72-3
butchery 17-23

calculators 32
Canterbury Tales (Middle English epic) 24-7, 29
cat o' nine tails (wicked whip) 59
Caxton, William (English printer) 11, 29-30, 124
Celtic (old language) 10, 14, 65
charms, lucky 74, 115
Chaucer, Geoffrey (English poet) 10, 24-9,
46, 98

chickens 57
    crossing 117
    not counting 108-9
Christmas Carol, A (Dickensian novel) 43-4
claptrap 86-7
class, social 133-4, 159, 182
codes 81, 114-16
Coleridge, Samuel Taylor (English poet) 163
computers, common 82, 86-7
curses, archaic 146-8

Dark Ages, diabolical 17-18
Dickens, Charles (English writer) 41-5, 48, 170
dictionaries 11-12, 36-7, 63-6, 85, 89-91, 138,
145, 180
    Webster's (of American English) 91, 138
dragons, daring 20

egress (exit) 33
Eliot, T.S. (Irish poet) 69
English 136, 141, 166
    American 48, 51, 56, 138, 148, 156-62
    Cockney 51, 135
    end of 182
    invaders 77
    language 89, 92, 95, 102, 119, 132-3
    Middle 10, 29, 31, 58, 100, 103-4, 135, 148
    Modern 30, 103, 148
    Old 10, 16-17, 24, 31, 33-4, 100, 103-4, 148
    Queen's 12
euphemisms, useful 45-53

exams, excruciating 187

fingers 32, 54, 56, 64, 110
foreign languages, fascinating 61-2, 125
forgeries, fraudulent 85
Franklin, Benjamin (American author) 180

gallows (murder machines) 6
games, great 63-71, 77, 90, 93-4, 111-12, 116-7
Gawain and the Green Knight (Old English epic) 20-1, 24
Gilbert and Sullivan (English songwriters) 23
graffiti (wrong writing) 71
grammar, gruesome 72-3
Greek (groovy language) 35, 37, 46, 55, 64, 117-18, 125, 132, 184
Gregory the Great (Pope) 15
guillotines (more murder machines) 42
Gutenberg, Johannes (German inventor) 10-11

hangings, horrific 41-2
heart, learning by 110
Henry III (English King) 38
Henry IV (English King) 10
Henry VIII (English King) 119
Homo sapiens, horrible 8
Hooligan, Patrick (Irish criminal) 34

initials, interesting 74, 80-2
insults 89, 106, 118, 135, 148, 186

jargon, jolly 82-8, 142
jeroboams (old toilets) 34
jesters 119
Johnson, Samuel (English writer) 12, 89-91, 145
jokes 11, 89, 106, 122
  knock-knock 92-4
  old 15, 117

practical 58-9
rude 119-20

knickers 35, 66, 148

Langland, John (English poet) 22, 24
language 7-8, 10-12, 61-2
  history of 13-16, 77-9, 99-104, 124-6, 156-62
Latin (lousy language) 10, 15-16, 32-3, 55, 74, 95, 113, 125, 132
lies 52-3

Macbeth (Shakespearean play) 129-31
McGonagall, William (Scottish poet) 166
magicians, meddling 69-70, 74
malapropisms (wrong words) 96-8
meringues, frightened 63
Middle Ages, measly 32, 46, 54, 58, 74-5, 92, 95, 114-15, 119, 133
Milne, A.A. (English writer) 112
monks 15-16, 19, 100-2, 183

National Curriculum 12
Neanderthals, no more 7-8
Normans, nasty 10, 99-104
notes, sick 85

Oliver Twist (Dickensian novel) 44
onomatopoeia 105-6

pangrams, playing with 68
Parliament 139, 145
poets 17-18, 163-8
Poets Laureate, prize-winning 164
Political Correctness (PC) 182-9
POSH (old acronym) 81, 134
printing press, proper 10-11, 29, 124
proverbs 28, 30, 53, 60, 88, 107-13, 123, 148, 155, 168

qabbalah, arcane 114-16

Renaissance, renewing 124-6
rhymes 22, 24, 120, 127, 132, 164
rhythms 127
riddles, ridiculous 117-23
robots (mechanical slaves) 37
Romans, rotten 10, 13-15, 32, 37, 55, 95, 118, 162
Romeo and Juliet (Shakespearean play) 51, 128

salaries, salty 55
sandwiches 35, 62
Shakespeare, William (English playwright) 11, 51, 97, 127-31, 140, 145, 150, 162
Sheridan, Richard (Irish playwright) 96
shocks, short sharp 23
sideburns, silly 37
slang, slobbish 12, 49-51, 65, 142-4, 148, 169, 171, 174
snobs, snooty 132-5
speech, figures of 54-60
spelling, simple 11-12, 30, 56, 72, 91-2, 102, 136-41
Spoonerisms, scrambled 149-52
stand, long 59
Stephen (English King) 100-2
supper, singing for 18

Tale of Two Cities, A (Dickensian novel) 42-3
taxis, tales about 37-8
teachers 8, 46, 48, 54, 63, 72, 74, 85, 89, 110, 112, 120, 122, 127, 132-3, 136, 138, 141-2, 156, 169, 185-8
Tell, William (Swiss freedom fighter) 57-8
Thatcher, Margaret (British Prime Minister) 39
timelines, tedious 10-12
tongue-twisters, tortuous 153-5
Trueman, Freddy (English cricketer) 23

unmentionables (don't ask) 46-7

verse 163-8
Victoria (British Queen) 39
Victorians, vile 23, 35, 41-2, 46, 121, 153
Vikings, vicious 10, 55, 77-9, 99
Vision of Piers Plowman (Old English epic) 22

whipping, words for 58-9
wicked, no peace for the 111
William the Conqueror (English King) 99-100, 103
wives, paying for 34
words 5-9, 182-9
    cross 176-9
    definitions 169-75
    long 132-3
    magic 35, 69, 74-6, 79, 114-16, 138
    new 37, 80, 124-7, 156, 160, 188-9
    no 130
    not hurting 117
    rude 10-12, 25, 35, 119-20, 145
    shocking 142, 145-8
    special-sounding 105-6
    swear 145-8
    twisted 153-5
    well-chosen 107-13
    of wisdom 28, 30, 53, 60, 88, 107-13, 123, 148, 155, 168
World War I (WWI), wasteful 34
World War II (WWII), woeful 51, 65, 82
writing 9, 12, 62-3, 85, 137
    wearing 74-5
    work for writers 11, 42, 45, 89, 127, 150, 164, 182

X-rays 39

yuppies, well-off 39-40